For Haruki and Yukito.
Cooking for you every day is a joy.

GOOD COOKING EVERY DAY

JULIA BUSUTTIL NISHIMURA

CONTENTS

INTRODUCTION

From when I was very young, I found great joy in choosing recipes from my mother's cookbooks. I relished spending my weekends immersed in their pages. I would write a list of everything I needed and scour the cupboards and fridge for anything we already had. We would walk to the local shops, list in hand, to collect any remaining ingredients needed. This love for planning and preparing meals was really nurtured throughout my childhood.

When I lived in Italy, I was inspired by the Italian way of eating. Every meal was something to celebrate – the first zucchini flowers at the market, a casual dinner with friends, a long birthday lunch in the garden. It didn't matter what the occasion, there was an unspoken pleasure in food and sharing it with others that was invigorating to be part of.

I kept a small red notebook during this time, where I would jot down things that captivated me – recipes from friends, dishes on menus, produce at markets and in delis. I wrote down everything I ate and cooked. I still have it and refer to it often.

And it was in Italy where I truly began to understand what most meals I enjoyed had in common: good-quality seasonal produce and simple cooking. There was always a flow and even if a meal was thrown together at the last minute, it always felt intentional.

Whether it is a celebratory feast or a simple weeknight dinner, choosing the dishes that complement each other for the moment is a wonderful thing. There are a few considerations that help me decide what to cook. Seasonality underpins everything. I rarely go to the shops with a list. I like to see what is on offer, then use that as a guide for my cooking. Planning and list-making are fine, too, but be prepared to be flexible. If something is not looking its best, make a change. It is far better to buy the best produce you can than to cook with out-of-season or less-than-ideal produce. Decades on, I still adore grocery shopping – produce is exciting. And while time constraints are often a factor in our busy lives, there is also a lot of pleasure to be found in the task.

As well as what is in season, my cooking is guided by a memory or mood or simply by what is in my pantry. It's important to think about how each ingredient and, in turn, each dish speaks to each other. No one thing should be the hero, outshining the others, but rather the aim is to create a harmonious balance of flavours, textures and feel. A menu is not a random group of dishes eaten one after the other, instead it is about cooking and eating with purpose. Whether the food is celebrating the season or taking you on a journey to a place where you once travelled, it is emotive and invigorating.

While each recipe in this book is a stand-alone dish – take, for example, the marinated spiced lamb with cucumber yoghurt (see page 134), perfect for a mid-week dinner, or the Roman stuffed tomatoes (see page 159), divine simply as they are – there are many dishes within these pages that marry together nicely to form a more complete larger meal. So, I have included a collection of menus (see pages 228– 253) that have significant meaning to me. And because cooking several dishes for one meal requires a little forward thinking and planning, I have thought carefully about how each menu might come together in your kitchen, too.

Before I even begin planning and cooking, I often visualise the dishes on the table and how they work with each other. This usually begins while I'm shopping at the market or grocer. Perhaps it is the small zucchini and bulging pods of broad beans that appear at the same time or the blood oranges, leaves still intact, alongside almost-too-pretty-to-eat radicchio, which inspire a meal. Large velvety green sage leaves jump out to me and implore me to cook with them, just as the sour cherries in my freezer from summer's picking invite me to bake a cake redolent of a slice enjoyed in a Roman trattoria in the late hours one evening.

You needn't look much farther than what is in season to help put a meal together. Fresh borlotti beans meet new crisp apples, which then meet chestnuts and celeriac, and before you blink you have everything you need for an elegant lunch. Ripe tomatoes, squishy from the hot sun, become a summery pasta, melons fragrant and sweet and cucumbers at their peak find their place in a lunch reminiscent of time spent in southern Italy. Each season is as exciting as the last and makes way for new recipes, opportunities and moments.

There is a menu for each time of the year and most occasions. The menus are simple but well thought out and yet there is much room for interpretation and interchangeability. I hope each menu will bring joy to your kitchen and mealtimes and I'm sure you will find new ways to combine the recipes in this book into meals and moments that will be just as meaningful to you.

DIS

HES

CHAPTER ONE

Bread, tarts & small things

PAGES 14–45

Every meal is something to celebrate – the first zucchini flowers at the market, a casual dinner with friends, a long birthday lunch in the garden.

SPRING BRUSCHETTA

Whenever I have friends over, I usually start with something on grilled bread. These bruschette are great because, if you use frozen peas, they are not just for spring, although eating them in spring does feel very right. The bread can be grilled and the topping made ahead of time, with assembly taking place just before serving.

- 350 g fresh shelled peas or frozen baby peas
- 2 garlic cloves
- juice of ½ lemon, plus extra juice and finely grated zest to serve
- handful each of mint leaves and parsley leaves
- 30 g Pecorino Romano, grated, plus extra to serve
- 80 ml (⅓ cup) extra-virgin olive oil, plus extra for drizzling
- sea salt and black pepper
- 4 slices of sourdough
- 2 × 100 g buffalo mozzarella balls, roughly torn, at room temperature
- 8 anchovy fillets in olive oil, drained

Blanch the peas until tender, drain and refresh under cold water. Reserve 50 g (⅓ cup) of the peas and set aside.

Finely grate one of the garlic cloves and place in a food processor with the peas, the lemon juice, mint, parsley and Pecorino Romano. Process to a fairly smooth mixture, scraping the side of the bowl if needed. Stream in the olive oil, process again to combine and season to taste. Transfer to a bowl and mix in the reserved peas. Set aside.

Grill both sides of the bread on a grill plate until golden and slightly charred on both sides. Halve the remaining garlic clove and rub one side of the grilled bread with the cut side of the garlic. Place the bread on a serving plate and drizzle with some extra olive oil. Top with some mozzarella, follow with a spoonful of the pea mixture and finish by draping over an anchovy fillet. Top with some lemon zest and extra lemon juice, another drizzle of olive oil, a scattering of extra Pecorino Romano and season with salt and pepper. Cut each slice in half to serve as a snack.

SERVES 8

MELON, MINT & PROSCIUTTO

A fresh food market is undoubtedly one of my favourite places to be, no matter where I am in the world. My friends Francesco and Julie took me to their local one in Altamura, Puglia, a town famous for many things, not least its bread. I am like a child at the market, full of wonder, talking to all the shopkeepers offering samples of their produce. I was so thrilled to try barattiere – a green fruit typical of the region, which has the taste of a melon but the freshness of a cucumber. It is delicate, mildly sweet and great as a snack or in salads. We ate it peeled and sliced, with good olive oil, mint and salt. So, while it might not be made with barattiere, this little snack is inspired by that time in Puglia and the classic combination of melon and prosciutto. I like to use Prosciutto di Parma or Prosciutto di San Daniele.

- ½ honeydew melon, skin and seeds removed, sliced into wedges
- small handful of mint leaves, finely sliced
- 2 tablespoons extra-virgin olive oil
- black pepper
- 6 slices of prosciutto crudo

Arrange the melon on a serving plate. Scatter with the mint leaves and drizzle with the olive oil. Season with the pepper, drape on the prosciutto and serve.

SERVES 4

FOCACCIA

WITH SWEET ONIONS & CHERRY TOMATO

There is a small forno (bakery) in the Pugliese town of Ostuni called Forno 31. Every morning I would meander through the small streets of the 'white city' from my holiday apartment to this sweetest little bakery, filled with locals. Get there too late and there would only be friselle and baked sweets to choose from (still a win), but get there early enough and I would be rewarded with oily and incredible still-warm focaccia – stuffed with sweet melty onions and cherry tomatoes – from the wood-fired oven. Wrapped in paper, soon to be transparent, I would walk back with this morsel, very satisfied and blissfully happy. Focaccia ripiena con la cipolla (stuffed focaccia with onions), made with sweet local onions, is a staple in Puglia, so although this recipe is not identical – it couldn't be – it is still joy filled, delicious and a good substitute for when I can't be at Forno 31.

- 3 tablespoons extra-virgin olive oil, plus extra for drizzling
- 4 onions (around 1 kg), finely sliced
- sea salt
- 300 g cherry tomatoes, halved
- 2 marjoram or oregano sprigs

FOCACCIA DOUGH

- 1 potato (around 150 g), peeled and quartered
- 250 g semolina flour (semola rimacinata)
- 250 g tipo 00 flour
- 5 g fine sea salt
- 5 g active dried yeast

For the focaccia dough, cook the potato in salted boiling water for 10–15 minutes or until cooked through. Drain and press through a potato ricer or mash. Transfer to the large bowl of a stand mixer fitted with the dough hook attachment, then add the remaining dough ingredients and 350 ml of warm water. Mix on a medium–high speed for 12–14 minutes or until the dough is elastic and not sticking to the side of the bowl. To check whether enough gluten has developed in the dough, stop the mixer and pull out a little piece of the dough. With both your hands, stretch it out. It should stretch without tearing until almost transparent. This is called the 'windowpane method'. Continue mixing and checking until you can create the 'windowpane' successfully. Drizzle the dough with a little olive oil and work the dough into a ball by folding it in on itself a few times. Cover with a damp tea towel and allow to rise at room temperature for 1 hour or until doubled in size.

Meanwhile, warm the olive oil in a large frying pan over a medium–low heat and add the onion along with a pinch of salt. Cook for 12–15 minutes or until the onion is softened and beginning to colour. Add the tomatoes and marjoram or oregano and cook for a further 20 minutes or until the tomatoes have broken down and the mixture is thick and rich. Season to taste with salt and allow to cool.

Preheat the oven to 200°C fan-forced. Grease a 30 cm × 25 cm × 2 cm baking tray with olive oil.

Punch down the dough and transfer it to a clean work surface. Split the dough into two pieces, one slightly larger than the other.

Place the larger piece of dough on the tray and use your fingers to press and stretch it out to cover the base of the tray. Spread the onion filling over the base, leaving a 2 cm border. Stretch out the second smaller piece of dough on the bench to roughly the size of the tray, then gently lift and ease the dough onto the filling, stretching it out to reach the corners. The dough will be quite thin at this point. Pinch the base and top together around the edges to seal. Drizzle with plenty of olive oil and allow to rest at room temperature for 30 minutes or until the dough is a little puffy and risen.

Bake the focaccia in the oven for 35–40 minutes or until golden and puffed. Allow to cool, then slice and serve.

SERVES 8

STILTON, ONION & SILVERBEET TART

One of my favourite cheeses is Stilton from Colston Bassett Dairy, Nottinghamshire. It is readily available at good cheesemongers and is beautifully savoury. I often buy too much to consume on a cheese board alone, and will add it to salads or crumble it into a rustic tart. Perfect for lunch, with some sharply dressed leaves, and sturdy in nature, this tart also travels well, making it ideal for a picnic.

- 1 egg, for egg wash

FLAKY PASTRY

- 250 g (1⅔ cups) plain flour, plus extra for dusting
- good pinch of sea salt
- 125 g cold unsalted butter, cubed
- 1 teaspoon white vinegar
- 80–100 ml iced water

FILLING

- 1 bunch of silverbeet, tough stems discarded
- 2 tablespoons extra-virgin olive oil
- 4 onions (around 1 kg), halved and finely sliced
- sea salt
- 100 ml pure cream
- 60 g pine nuts, toasted
- 125 g Stilton, crumbled
- ¼ teaspoon freshly grated nutmeg
- black pepper

For the flaky pastry, mix the flour and salt together in a large bowl. Use your fingertips to rub the butter into the flour to create flat pieces of butter coated by the flour. For a flaky dough, it is important not to overmix the butter. Drizzle in the vinegar and enough of the iced water to just bring the dough together (you might not need all of it). It will still be shaggy, but should hold together when pressed. If there are dry or floury spots, sprinkle in a little more water, a teaspoon at a time, until the dough just comes together. Flatten into a thick disc about 10–12 cm in diameter, wrap in plastic wrap or baking paper and refrigerate for at least 1 hour.

For the filling, blanch the silverbeet in a large saucepan of salted boiling water for 1–2 minutes or until vibrant and just cooked. Drain, refresh in iced water and squeeze out the excess water. Roughly chop and place in a large bowl. Warm the olive oil in a large frying pan over a medium–low heat and add the onion with a pinch of salt. Cook the onion, stirring occasionally, for 12–15 minutes or until it is very soft and beginning to caramelise. Add to the bowl with the silverbeet and allow to cool. Once the silverbeet mixture is cool, add all the remaining filling ingredients and mix to combine. Season well and set aside.

Preheat the oven to 190°C fan-forced. Line a 30 cm round baking tray with baking paper and set aside.

Remove the dough from the fridge and let it sit at room temperature for 10 minutes to make it easier to roll. Roll out the dough on a lightly floured work surface to form a large disc, about 3 mm thick, massaging the edge as you roll to prevent it from cracking too much. Drape the pastry over the tray. Spread the filling mixture onto the pastry, leaving a 5 cm border. Fold the pastry edge towards the centre of the tart, pinching as you go to seal in the filling and form a galette.

Whisk the egg with 1 teaspoon of water in a small bowl, then brush the egg wash over the pastry. Bake the tart for 45–50 minutes or until the pastry is golden. Allow to cool for 15 minutes before serving.

SERVES 6–8

SESAME FLATBREAD

Rolled in sesame seeds, these flatbreads are light, fluffy and versatile. I like to top them with labneh, tomatoes and cucumber for a simple lunch, or serve them, to be torn and dipped, with the herby tahini dip on page 28. They are a staple in my kitchen and can be made without sesame seeds, of course, but I love how nutty the seeds become once cooked.

350 g tipo 00 flour, plus extra for rolling and dusting
150 g semolina flour
5 g fine sea salt
7 g active dried yeast
extra-virgin olive oil, for drizzling
80 g white untoasted sesame seeds, for sprinkling
flaky sea salt, to serve

Place the flours, salt and yeast in the large bowl of a stand mixer fitted with the dough hook attachment. Pour in 350 ml of warm water and mix on a medium–high speed for 12–14 minutes or until the dough is elastic and not sticking to the side of the bowl. To check whether enough gluten has developed in the dough, stop the mixer and pull out a little piece of the dough. With both your hands, stretch it out. It should stretch without tearing until almost transparent. This is called the 'windowpane method'. Continue mixing and checking until you can create the 'windowpane' successfully.

Drizzle the dough with a little olive oil and work the dough into a ball by folding it in on itself a few times. Cover with a damp tea towel and allow to rise at room temperature for 1 hour or until doubled in size.

Punch down the dough and turn out onto a clean work surface. Divide the dough into six equal pieces and roll into balls. Dust with a little extra flour, cover with a damp tea towel and allow to rise again for 45 minutes or until puffy and risen.

Sprinkle a layer of sesame seeds onto a plate.

Roll the balls of dough into discs, around 15 cm in diameter. Press the discs into the sesame seeds on one side only.

Working with one at a time, cook the flatbreads, sesame seed–side down first, in a large frying pan over a medium–high heat for 30 seconds to 1 minute, or until the seeds are golden. Flip and cook the flatbreads for a further 2–3 minutes, until golden and puffy.

Serve the flatbreads drizzled with a little extra olive oil and a sprinkle of flaky sea salt.

SERVES 6

TAHINI HERB DIP

- 1 bunch of parsley, leaves and stalks
- 1 bunch of coriander, leaves and stalks
- 1 garlic clove
- 1 long green chilli, seeds removed
- 100 g hulled tahini
- 200 g full-fat Greek yoghurt
- juice of 1 lemon
- 2 tablespoons extra-virgin olive oil
- pinch of saffron threads
- sea salt

Without the yoghurt, I originally made this sauce – brimming with flavour, a little kick from the chilli and freshness from plenty of herbs – to serve with lamb cutlets or grilled chicken. With the yoghurt added, it becomes this creamy bright mixture, perfect as a dip to serve with my sesame flatbread on page 27 or raw vegetables.

Place the parsley, coriander, garlic, chilli and tahini in a food processor or blender. Blitz until a fairly fine consistency. Add the yoghurt and lemon juice and continue to blitz until well combined.

Transfer the tahini herb dip to a bowl, stir through the olive oil and saffron, and season to taste with salt.

SERVES 4–6

TOMATOES ON TOAST

A warm day in Rome saw me in a taxi on my way to an unassuming piazza in Appio-Latino. The destination was SantoPalato, the uber-cool trattoria headed up by Sarah Cicolini. The first thing I ordered was the bruschetta, pomodoro e formaggio – a ridiculously good piece of grilled bread smothered in tomatoes and topped with a firm goat's cheese. Inspired partly by this lunch and partly by the classic Catalan dish of pan con tomate (pa amb tomàquet), comes my tomatoes on toast. With so few ingredients, it is imperative that you buy the best-quality ingredients you can for this very simple dish.

- 6 slices of sourdough bread
- ½ garlic clove
- 500 g ripe tomatoes
- 2 tablespoons extra-virgin olive oil, plus extra for drizzling
- 2 marjoram sprigs, leaves picked
- sea salt and black pepper
- 6 anchovy fillets in olive oil, drained
- 80 g surface-ripened goat's cheese, sliced

Grill both sides of the bread on a grill plate until toasted and beginning to char. Rub one side of the grilled bread with the cut side of the garlic. Set aside.

Grate the tomatoes on the coarse side of a box grater. Drain the tomato pulp in a sieve to reduce the amount of liquid, then place in a bowl with the olive oil and marjoram and season to taste. Mix well with a spoon.

Halve the grilled bread and drizzle generously with some extra olive oil. Top with the tomato mixture and season. Then top half of the toasts with the anchovy fillets and the other half with the goat's cheese and serve.

SERVES 6

ROAST CARROT & HARISSA TART

I love making pastry and I am always thinking up new things I can turn into a tart or pie. One drizzly wintry day, I bought some beautiful carrots at the market and had a craving for something comforting. I had originally planned to make a tarte tatin, but settled instead on a beautiful free-form tart. I decided the carrots would be more flavourful this way. They pair so wonderfully with the harissa, which you can increase or reduce, depending on your preference, and it is all complemented by a little herb salad and some crème fraîche. Top the tart just before serving.

- 900 g carrots of varying colours, trimmed
- 1 tablespoon extra-virgin olive oil
- 1 tablespoon honey
- 1 teaspoon fennel seeds
- 1 teaspoon red wine vinegar
- sea salt
- 1 tablespoon unsalted butter
- 1 tablespoon harissa paste (or homemade, see page 33)
- 1 egg, for egg wash
- 100 g labneh (or homemade, see page 214), to serve

FLAKY PASTRY

- 250 g plain flour
- 125 g cold unsalted butter, cubed
- good pinch of sea salt
- 1 teaspoon white vinegar
- 80–100 ml iced water

HERB SALAD

- small handful each of dill fronds and parsley leaves, roughly torn
- 40 g walnuts, toasted and roughly chopped
- 1 shallot, finely sliced
- 1 tablespoon extra-virgin olive oil
- juice of ½ lemon
- sea salt and black pepper

Preheat the oven to 185°C fan-forced. Line a baking tray with baking paper.

Cut the carrots in half lengthways, then into halves crossways. Place in a large bowl and add the olive oil, honey, fennel seeds and red wine vinegar. Season to taste with salt and mix well to coat the carrots. Tip the carrots, along with any liquid, onto the tray. Dot the carrots with the butter and roast for 35–40 minutes or until the carrots are cooked through and nicely caramelised. Spoon on the harissa and toss to coat. Set aside to cool.

Meanwhile, for the flaky pastry, mix the flour and salt together in a large bowl. Use your fingertips to rub the butter into the flour to create flat pieces of butter coated by the flour. For a flaky dough, it is important not to overmix the butter. Drizzle in the vinegar and enough of the iced water to just bring the dough together (you might not need all of it). It will still be shaggy, but should hold together when pressed. If there are dry or floury spots, sprinkle in a little more water, a teaspoon at a time, until the dough just comes together. Flatten into a thick disc about 10–12 cm in diameter, wrap and refrigerate for at least 1 hour.

Line a 30 cm round baking tray with baking paper.

Remove the dough from the fridge and let it sit at room temperature for 10 minutes to make it easier to roll. Roll out the dough on a lightly floured work surface to form a large disc, about 3 mm thick, massaging the edge as you roll to prevent it from cracking too much. Drape the pastry over the tray. Arrange the carrot mixture on the pastry, leaving a 5 cm border. Fold the pastry edge towards the centre of the tart, pinching as you go to seal in the filling and form a galette. Refrigerate for 30 minutes.

Increase the oven temperature to 190°C fan-forced.

Whisk the egg with 1 teaspoon of water in a small bowl, then brush the egg wash over the pastry. Bake the tart for 45–50 minutes or until the pastry is cooked through and nicely golden. Allow to cool for 15 minutes.

While the tart is cooling, make the herb salad by combining the dill, parsley, walnuts and shallot in a small bowl. Drizzle on the olive oil and lemon juice and season to taste.

Spoon the labneh over the tart filling, top with the herb salad and serve.

SERVES 4–6

HARISSA

Harissa is a North African spicy chilli paste and such a versatile condiment. It's smoky and fragrant, with a deep, rich flavour. I make a jar of it most weeks as I love having it in the fridge to serve with grilled meats or fish, but also with roasted vegetables or on top of salads with some canned fish.

- 5 long red chillies
- 2 long red capsicums
- 3 garlic cloves, crushed with the side of a knife
- 2 teaspoons cumin seeds, toasted and coarsely crushed
- 2 teaspoons coriander seeds, toasted and coarsely crushed
- 2 teaspoons Aleppo pepper
- juice of 1 lemon
- 2 tablespoons extra-virgin olive oil
- sea salt

Cook the chillies and capsicums on a grill (or roast them in a hot oven) until blackened all over. Remove from the heat and place in a bowl. Cover with a plate and allow to cool briefly. When cool enough to touch, remove the skin from the chillies, then cut away the stem and discard. Place in a food processor. Peel the skin from the capsicums and discard, along with the seeds and any membrane. Place the flesh in the food processor and add the garlic, cumin and coriander seeds, and Aleppo pepper. Blitz until coarsely chopped. Stream in the lemon juice and olive oil and continue to process until you have a fairly smooth paste. (I like to leave my harissa with a little bit of texture, so towards the end I tend to pulse rather than blitz.) Season to taste and transfer to a jar. Harissa will keep in the fridge for up to a week.

MAKES APPROXIMATELY 200 G

Recipe images overleaf

PIZZA BIANCA

One of my favourite places in Rome to pick up a slice of pizza bianca or rossa is Antico Forno Roscioli, a busy and bustling spot. Sold by weight, they will hold up a pizza and use their knife to gesture how big you want the piece to be. In return you gesture back with your hands – a 'this much' signal. It's a dance between customer and server, which I just love. Although pizza bianca translates to 'white pizza', it is more of a bread or focaccia than a pizza. It's chewy, a little crispy and delicious split in half and stuffed with whatever takes your fancy. I love it filled simply with finely sliced mortadella, but buffalo mozzarella, basil and tomato or salami and stracchino are great, too.

No need for any fancy equipment here, just your hands and some time are all you require. Be very gentle once the dough has undergone its long rising time – you want to preserve all the bubbles in the dough, which are what make pizza bianca so special.

- 500 g tipo 0 flour
- 400 ml iced water
- 5 g active dried yeast
- 5 g honey
- 2 teaspoons extra-virgin olive oil, plus extra for drizzling
- 5 g fine sea salt
- flaky sea salt, for topping
- finely sliced mortadella or your choice of filling, to serve (optional)

Place the flour in a large bowl and make a well in the centre. Slowly pour in 200 ml of the iced water. Add the yeast, honey and olive oil and begin to mix the flour into the water with your hands. Add 150 ml of the remaining iced water and work the dough. Add the fine salt, then pour in the remaining water and continue to work the dough until it is sticky and smooth, around 5–6 minutes.

Turn the dough out onto a clean work surface and work the dough in a slapping and folding motion. It will be quite sticky to begin with and a little difficult to work, but as the gluten develops, the dough will change in appearance and become more elastic. Depending on how hard and fast you work the dough, this can take anywhere from 5–10 minutes.

Transfer the dough to a well-oiled bowl and cover with a damp tea towel. Allow to rise at room temperature for 8–12 hours or until light and bubbly. If it is a particularly hot day, keep an eye on the dough as it rises and reduce this time as needed.

Prepare a large tray by drizzling with olive oil.

Very gently divide the dough into two. Shape the pieces into plump oval shapes and transfer to the tray. Drizzle with more olive oil, gently rub the oil onto the dough, then add a sprinkling of flaky salt. Allow to rise at room temperature for a further 25–30 minutes.

Preheat the oven to 250°C fan-forced. Place a 40 cm × 20 cm baking tray in the oven to heat up.

Gently lift one of the dough pieces onto a clean work surface greased with olive oil and dimple the dough with your fingertips, gently stretching it out as you press into it and form a shape similar to the tray. It should be around 1 cm thick once stretched, but if the dough doesn't stretch to cover the entire tray, that is fine, too.

Transfer the dough to the preheated tray and cook until the pizza bianca is golden and crunchy on the bottom, around 12 minutes. Repeat with the second piece of dough.

Top the pizza bianca with more olive oil and cut into squares to serve with a meal or slice in half, horizontally, and fill with the mortadella or filling of your choice.

MAKES 2 LARGE PIZZE

TOMATO TART

WITH CAPERS & HERBS

Towards the end of summer, when tomatoes are at their best, I make this tart at least once a week. Not only is it incredibly simple and beautiful, the combination of tomatoes, goat's curd and capers is really formidable. The pastry has some rye flour in there, which gives a nice nuttiness to this tart. If you can't find goat's curd, some soft goat's cheese crumbled on top would also be nice. Served outdoors in the early evening, this tart is one for the season.

- 800 g tomatoes, cut into 6–8 mm thick slices
- 3 oregano sprigs, leaves picked
- extra-virgin olive oil, for drizzling
- sea salt and black pepper
- 1 egg, for egg wash
- large handful of parsley leaves, finely chopped
- large handful of mint leaves, finely chopped
- 2 tablespoons capers, rinsed and patted dry, roughly chopped
- 100 g goat's curd

FLAKY PASTRY

- 200 g plain flour, plus extra for dusting
- 50 g rye (or wholemeal) flour
- good pinch of sea salt
- 125 g cold unsalted butter, cubed
- 1 teaspoon white vinegar
- 60–80 ml iced water

For the pastry, mix the flours and salt together in a large bowl. Use your fingertips to rub the butter into the flour to create flat pieces of butter coated by the flour. For a flaky dough, it is important not to overmix the butter. Drizzle in the vinegar and enough of the iced water to just bring the dough together (you might not need all of it). It will still be shaggy, but should hold together when pressed and not be dry or floury. If there are dry or floury spots, sprinkle in a little more water, a teaspoon at a time, until the dough just comes together. Flatten into a thick disc about 10–12 cm in diameter, wrap in plastic wrap or baking paper and refrigerate for at least 1 hour.

Preheat the oven to 190°C fan-forced. Line a 30 cm round baking tray with baking paper.

Remove the dough from the fridge and let it sit at room temperature for 10 minutes to make it easier to roll. Roll out the dough on a lightly floured work surface to form a large disc, about 3 mm thick, massaging the edge as you roll to prevent it from cracking too much. Drape the pastry over the tray.

Arrange the tomato slices on the pastry, leaving a 5 cm border, then add the oregano leaves, tucking them in around the tomato. Drizzle with some olive oil and season with salt and pepper. Fold the pastry towards the centre of the tart, pinching as you go to seal in the filling and form a galette.

Whisk the egg with 1 teaspoon of water in a small bowl, then brush the egg wash over the pastry. Bake the tart for 45 minutes or until the pastry is golden and the tomatoes are well cooked. Allow to cool. Top the tart with the parsley, mint, capers and goat's curd. Drizzle with a little more olive oil, season to taste and serve.

SERVES 6–8

MOZZARELLA, CRÈME FRAÎCHE

& BOILED LEMON

I first read about boiled lemons in a newspaper article featuring Claudia Roden quite a few years ago. I had never come across this method before and it was a revelation. Boiled for around 30 minutes in salted water, the lemons become soft and far less bitter, resembling a preserved lemon, except in my opinion, rather nicer. You can use the flesh and the skin, chopped up and added to marinades, stews or even salads. I like to include it here in this simple dish of marinated mozzarella. It makes for a wonderful snack or starter. Sometimes I also add some blanched and podded broad beans, or mint or basil. It is an ingenious way to use lemon, I think.

- 1 lemon
- sea salt
- 3 × 100 g buffalo mozzarella balls, roughly torn or thickly sliced, at room temperature
- 200 g crème fraîche
- black pepper
- extra-virgin olive oil, for drizzling

Place the lemon in a small saucepan and cover with water. Season with salt and bring to the boil. Boil for 30 minutes or until the lemon is soft. Allow the lemon to cool in the water, then drain. Cut the lemon in half and set one half aside for another use. Scoop out the flesh of the remaining half and roughly chop. Place in a bowl. Finely chop half of the hollowed-out skin and add to the flesh. Finely slice the remaining skin and set aside for serving.

Add the mozzarella and crème fraîche to the bowl with the lemon. Mix gently. Season to taste with salt and pepper and arrange on a serving plate. Drizzle with plenty of olive oil and top with the reserved sliced lemon skin.

SERVES 6

POACHED & MARINATED PRAWNS

- 1 celery stalk, halved crossways
- 3 black peppercorns
- 1 shallot, halved and unpeeled
- 2 marjoram or oregano sprigs
- 1 fresh bay leaf
- 2 slices of lemon
- sea salt
- 16 large raw prawns

MARINADE

- 125 ml (½ cup) extra-virgin olive oil
- 1 lemon, ½ finely sliced, ½ juiced
- handful of parsley leaves, finely chopped
- handful of mint leaves, finely chopped
- ½ long red chilli, seeds removed, sliced
- sea salt and black pepper

These poached and marinated prawns, inspired by a Marcella Hazan recipe, are my go-to for any kind of celebration or long lunch. Impressive, yet simple, they are such a wonderful way to serve prawns, and the marinade is actually marvellous with grilled squid or even with fish, too. You can make this dish ahead of time, just be sure to bring the prawns to room temperature before serving. Plenty of bread to mop up all the delicious marinade is a must.

Place the celery, peppercorns, shallot, marjoram or oregano, bay leaf and lemon slices in a large saucepan. Cover with 2 litres of cold water and season well with salt. Bring to the boil, then reduce the heat to low and add the prawns. Gently poach the prawns for 4–5 minutes or until they are just cooked. Remove the prawns and, when cool enough to handle, peel and devein them, discarding the heads and shells.

Transfer the prawns to a shallow bowl and add the marinade ingredients. Stir to coat and set aside to marinate for 15 minutes, before serving at room temperature. Alternatively, make ahead and refrigerate, then bring to room temperature before serving.

SERVES 4

HALOUMI, FETA & SILVERBEET PIE

After a trip to my local Greek deli, I came home with too much of everything – haloumi, feta, olives and various jarred goods. Having too much of things often inspires new recipes, as I look to create something to utilise my haul. On this particular occasion it was this pie, filled with feta and haloumi and silverbeet from my garden. I was out of butter and so I made an olive oil pastry. It is such a reliable and forgiving dough, coming together very simply and easily able to be rolled out and stretched. The top layer is rolled out until almost transparent, creating a thin and crisp pastry once cooked. This pie is utterly delightful and left on the bench, will disappear very quickly.

- 1 bunch of silverbeet, tough stems discarded
- 2 spring onions, finely sliced
- 2 teaspoons dried mint
- 1 tablespoon za'atar
- large handful of parsley leaves, finely chopped
- large handful of dill fronds, finely chopped
- finely grated zest of 1 lemon
- 200 g haloumi, coarsely grated
- 150 g Greek feta, crumbled
- sea salt and black pepper

OLIVE OIL PASTRY

- 300 g tipo 00 flour, plus extra for dusting
- 2½ tablespoons extra-virgin olive oil, plus extra for greasing and drizzling
- 5 g fine sea salt

For the olive oil pastry, combine the flour, olive oil and salt with 150 ml of water in the large bowl of a stand mixer fitted with the dough hook attachment. Mix on a medium speed for 8–10 minutes or until the dough is strong and elastic. Wrap tightly with plastic wrap or place in an airtight container where it will fit snugly and rest at room temperature for 1 hour.

Blanch the silverbeet in a large saucepan of salted boiling water for 2–3 minutes. Drain and, when cool enough to touch, squeeze out as much water as possible. You will need around 150 g of cooked silverbeet. Roughly chop the cooked silverbeet, place in a bowl with the remaining ingredients and mix well. Taste, adjust the seasoning if needed and set aside.

Preheat the oven to 200°C fan-forced. Grease a 30 cm × 25 cm × 2 cm baking tray with olive oil and set aside.

Tip the rested dough onto a clean work surface and divide the dough into two. Working with one piece of dough at a time, roll out the dough as thinly as possible, using your hands to help stretch it by gently lifting and pulling the edges. If the dough is too sticky, dust with a little extra flour to help roll it out. Carefully drape the rolled dough onto the tray, allowing the excess to overhang, then gently spread the filling onto the dough all the way to the edge.

Repeat the rolling and stretching with the second piece of dough and drape it over the filling. Trim any thick edges of dough, ensuring there is at least 2 cm of overhanging dough to work with. Press the edges together to seal, then fold into the centre of the pie, crimping the dough as you work around the edges. Brush with more olive oil, sprinkle over some salt and bake for 35–40 minutes or until the pastry is golden. Allow to cool briefly, then cut into squares and serve.

SERVES 4–6

CHAPTER TWO

Comforting soups

PAGES 46–65

Whether a meal is celebrating the season or taking you on a journey to a place where you once travelled, it should be emotive and invigorating.

KUSKSU

MALTESE SPRING SOUP

On a recent trip to Malta, I was invited to lunch by well-known Maltese cook Pippa Mattei. When I arrived at her home, I was greeted with warmth and the aroma of the Maltese spring soup kusksu on the stove. Fresh ġbejniet (Maltese cheeselets) were draining in their baskets and ħobż biż-żejt (open sandwiches; on this occasion, Maltese bread rubbed with ripe tomatoes and drizzled with plenty of good olive oil) were being made at the table. After some Maltese coffee and biscuits for morning tea, we went outside to eat in the garden. The kusksu was for lunch and every mouthful felt so familiar and comforting. Dessert was imqaret (fried date pastries) served with ice cream, honey and orange-blossom water. The perfect lunch. My cousin, Joanna, joined me for lunch that day and later shared with me her own recipe for kusksu. This is my version. The pasta is rather difficult to find outside Malta, so can be substituted with fregola, pearl couscous or any small pasta shape.

Making ġbejniet is simple, but a spoonful of ricotta dolloped into the soup is a fine substitute if you don't have the time or equipment.

- 2 tablespoons extra-virgin olive oil, plus extra for drizzling
- 1 tablespoon unsalted butter
- 2 garlic cloves, crushed with the side of a knife
- 2 tablespoons kunserva (Maltese tomato paste, see Note)
- 1 litre vegetable or chicken stock, plus more as needed
- 125 g kusksu pasta (piombino pasta shape)
- 700 g broad beans (200 g shelled)
- 400 g fresh peas in pods (150 g shelled)
- large handful of parsley leaves, finely chopped
- sea salt and black pepper
- 6 fresh ġbejniet (see page 51) or 250 g fresh ricotta, to serve
- grated Pecorino Romano, to serve

NOTE

Kunserva is a little sweeter than Italian tomato paste and can be purchased at some grocers and delis or at Maltese specialty shops. If unavailable, simply substitute with Italian tomato paste.

Warm the olive oil, butter and garlic in a large saucepan over a medium heat. When the garlic begins to sizzle, add the kunserva and stir to coat the garlic. Cook out the kunserva for 1 minute, then pour in the stock. Bring to a simmer, scatter in the kusksu pasta and cook for 10 minutes.

Add the shelled broad beans and peas to the pan and continue to cook until the pasta is al dente and the broad beans and peas are tender. Finish with the parsley and season to taste. The soup should be quite thick, but if it dries out too much, simply add a little more stock or water while it cooks.

Ladle the soup into bowls and place a ġbejniet or spoonful of ricotta in the centre. Drizzle with plenty of extra olive oil, scatter on the grated Pecorino Romano and top with a crack of black pepper.

SERVES 6

ĠBEJNIET

MALTESE SOFT CHEESELETS

Ġbejniet are well loved in Maltese cooking. Traditionally made in reed baskets called qwieleb, nowadays plastic cheese baskets are more often used to make these soft cheeses. I love them fresh, with some crusty bread and good olive oil, but they are also eaten hard – either sun dried or salt cured and then seasoned with herbs or rolled in cracked black pepper. My parents loved the pepper ones and there was always an oversized jar of them in our pantry, where they would sit in a vinegar solution to preserve them. Sliced and eaten for breakfast with bread and oil, or as part of a classic Maltese antipasto-style platter (platt Malti) it's well worth making them if you can. Although they are best made with sheep's or goat's milk, full-cream cow's milk is the next best thing. I use calcium chloride to help produce a firmer curd (an essential addition when using homogenised milk), then add liquid vegetarian rennet. Both are available from cheesemaking supplies stores. If the latter is unavailable, use a powdered rennet and follow the manufacturer's directions for the correct rennet-to-milk ratio.

- 2 litres full-cream cow's, goat's or sheep's milk
- 0.5 ml calcium chloride (50% solution)
- 0.5 ml liquid vegetarian rennet (200 IMCU/ml)
- non-iodised cheese salt, for sprinkling

Warm the milk, constantly stirring, in a large saucepan over a medium heat to 38°C on an instant-read thermometer. Remove from the heat.

Place a spoonful of the warm milk in a bowl. Add the calcium chloride and mix thoroughly to dilute the solution. Pour the calcium chloride mixture into the pan and stir. Repeat this process with the rennet. Pour the rennet mixture into the milk mixture and stir for 2 minutes. Cover with a lid and allow to sit for 45–60 minutes.

Place eight 7 cm × 6 cm cheese baskets on a wire rack set over a tray.

Cut the curds with a knife, then scoop them into the cheese baskets, filling them right to the top. Sprinkle with some salt and allow to drain for 1–2 hours. Flip the cheeses over and back into the baskets, sprinkle with salt and allow to drain overnight in the fridge. Turn the ġbejniet out and serve. The fresh ġbejniet can be stored in an airtight container in the fridge for up to 3 days.

MAKES 8 CHEESELETS

Recipe images overleaf

CHICKPEA & PORK SOUP

This very simple and warming soup, where the chickpeas and pork cook together with vegetables to create a flavour-filled broth, is the type of soup my mum made when I was younger; frugal yet so luxurious at the same time. It is perfect to make when it's raining outside and you have nowhere to be. The soup happily simmers away while you tend to other things. It really is necessary to use dried chickpeas here, as they help create the flavour for the broth as they cook.

- 250 g dried chickpeas
- 500 g thickly sliced bone-in pork belly rashers, cut into 6 cm pieces
- 1 tomato, quartered
- 2 celery stalks, roughly chopped
- 1 large carrot, halved lengthways, then halved crossways
- 1 potato, peeled and halved
- 2 sage sprigs
- 2 fresh bay leaves
- sea salt and black pepper
- roughly chopped parsley leaves, to serve

The night before you want to make the soup, place the chickpeas in a large bowl and cover with plenty of cold water. Allow to soak overnight.

Drain and rinse the chickpeas and transfer to a large saucepan, along with the pork, tomato, celery, carrot, potato, sage and bay leaves. Cover with 3 litres of water and bring to the boil over a high heat. Reduce the heat to medium–low and simmer for 1½–2 hours or until the chickpeas are very tender and the pork is soft. Skim any impurities that rise to the surface, especially during the first 30 minutes of cooking. Season to taste and break up any of the vegetables that are still large. Remove the pork from the bone and return the meat to the soup before serving.

Ladle the soup into bowls, top with the parsley and serve.

SERVES 6

CHESTNUT, RICE & PORCINI MINESTRA

This soup is on repeat during the cooler months. If you can find fresh chestnuts, they are exceptional here, but good-quality already cooked and peeled ones make light work of the task. I adore rice in soups – it's forever comforting and nourishing. Omit the pancetta and use vegetable stock to make this vegetarian.

- 350 g fresh chestnuts or 180 g peeled and cooked chestnuts, roughly chopped
- 8 g dried porcini
- 1.5 litres hot water
- 2 tablespoons extra-virgin olive oil, plus extra for drizzling
- 1 onion, finely diced
- 1 celery stalk, finely diced
- 150 g flat pancetta, cut into lardons
- 2 potatoes (such as Dutch cream or nicola), peeled and cut into 4 cm pieces
- 500 ml (2 cups) chicken stock
- 2 fresh bay leaves
- 150 g Carnaroli rice or other risotto rice
- sea salt and black pepper
- roughly chopped parsley leaves, to serve

If using fresh chestnuts, make a cross in the side of each chestnut with a sharp knife, then cook in a saucepan of salted boiling water for 15–20 minutes or until tender. Allow to cool, then peel and roughly chop. Set aside.

Meanwhile, place the porcini in a large bowl and cover with the hot water. Allow to steep for 15 minutes.

Warm the olive oil in a large saucepan over a medium–low heat. Add the onion, celery and pancetta and cook until the onion and celery are softened and the pancetta is starting to colour. Add the potato and cook for 3–4 minutes or until beginning to soften around the edges.

Add the chestnuts, the porcini and its strained soaking liquid, the stock and bay leaves to the pan. Simmer for 15 minutes or until slightly reduced. Scatter in the rice and cook for a further 15–20 minutes or until the rice is al dente. Season to taste and serve the minestra with a scattering of parsley and a drizzle of extra olive oil.

SERVES 6

ZUCCHINI, BASIL & FENNEL SOUP

Although perhaps not the first thing that comes to mind in summer, the produce of the season – think zucchini, tomatoes and corn – really is so wonderful in soups. This soup is light, creamy, fresh and pure – tasting of all the ingredients. Without the fried zucchini flowers, this soup of zucchini, basil and crème fraîche is still a total triumph. But I just cannot get past the gorgeousness of the flowers when they are in season and look for any way to use them. They sit on top in all their crunchy glory like a crouton, and are the perfect complement to the smooth soup underneath.

- 2 tablespoons extra-virgin olive oil, plus extra for drizzling
- 4 shallots, finely chopped
- 4 garlic cloves, roughly chopped
- ½ teaspoon fennel seeds, toasted
- sea salt
- 1 fennel bulb, fronds reserved, roughly chopped
- 800 g zucchini, roughly chopped
- 1 litre chicken or vegetable stock
- small handful of basil leaves
- 100 g crème fraîche, plus extra to serve
- black pepper

TEMPURA ZUCCHINI FLOWERS

- 100 ml sparkling water
- 3–4 ice cubes
- 65 g plain flour
- neutral vegetable oil, for frying
- 4 female zucchini flowers, stamens discarded

Warm the olive oil in a large saucepan over a medium–low heat. Gently cook the shallot, garlic and fennel seeds with a pinch of salt for 8–10 minutes or until the shallot and garlic are softened and beginning to colour. Increase the heat to medium, add the fennel and zucchini and cook for a further 5 minutes or until the vegetables begin to soften. Cover with the stock and simmer for 30–35 minutes or until the zucchini and fennel are tender. In the last 5 minutes, add the basil.

Use a stick blender to puree the soup or transfer to a blender and process until smooth. If using a blender, return the soup to the pan. Spoon in the crème fraîche, bring to a simmer over a medium heat and check for seasoning. Keep warm.

For the tempura zucchini flowers, place the sparkling water and ice cubes in a bowl. Add the flour and gently mix (chopsticks work well). Don't overmix the batter, lumps are totally fine. Set aside.

Pour enough vegetable oil into a wok or saucepan to come 6–7 cm up the side and heat to 190°C or until a little of the batter dropped in the oil browns in 10 seconds. Dip a zucchini flower in the batter, shake off the excess and lower into the hot oil. Repeat with another zucchini flower, being careful not to overcrowd the pan. Fry, turning once, until very lightly golden, around 2 minutes. Drain on a wire rack and sprinkle with a little salt. Repeat this process with the remaining zucchini flowers.

Ladle the hot soup into bowls and top with a tempura zucchini flower, a dollop of extra crème fraîche and the reserved fennel fronds. Drizzle with a little extra olive oil and crack over some pepper, then serve.

SERVES 4

PUMPKIN & SAGE SOUP

WITH MASCARPONE

If you see beautiful heirloom varieties of pumpkin in autumn, this is the recipe for them, particularly the Musquee de Provence variety. Its flesh is dense and a deep orange with a sweet flavour, almost with a scent of nutmeg. The result is a soup that is incredibly orange in colour and beautifully perfumed. While roasting the pumpkin is an extra step, I do think it is worth it. I don't like to blitz the soup, but rather leave the pumpkin to cook down in the stock, which gives a rough yet pleasing consistency. Topped with crispy sage leaves, mascarpone and Parmigiano Reggiano, this soup is heavenly and a true celebration of the season.

- 2 kg pumpkin, cut into 5–7 cm chunks
- 120 ml extra-virgin olive oil, plus extra for drizzling
- sea salt and black pepper
- 1 onion, roughly chopped
- 2 carrots, roughly chopped
- 2 garlic cloves, roughly chopped
- small handful of sage leaves
- 1 litre light chicken stock
- ¼ teaspoon freshly grated nutmeg

TO SERVE

- mascarpone
- finely grated Parmigiano Reggiano
- grilled bread

Preheat the oven to 180°C fan-forced. Line a baking tray with baking paper.

Arrange the pumpkin on the tray and drizzle on 2 tablespoons of the olive oil. Season and roast for 1 hour, turning the pumpkin over halfway, until cooked through and beginning to caramelise. Scoop out the flesh, discard the skin, and set aside.

Meanwhile, warm another 2 tablespoons of olive oil in a large saucepan over a medium heat and add the onion, carrot, garlic, two sage leaves and a good pinch of salt. Cook for 15–20 minutes or until the vegetables are very soft and beginning to colour.

Add the roasted pumpkin to the pan, along with the stock and nutmeg. Bring to a simmer and cook for 10 minutes or until the soup is thick and fairly smooth.

Heat the remaining 2 tablespoons of olive oil in a small frying pan over a medium heat and add the remaining sage leaves. Cook for around 2 minutes or until deep golden in colour and crisp. Drain on paper towel.

Ladle the soup into bowls and top with a dollop of mascarpone, a generous drizzle of extra olive oil, a scattering of grated Parmigiano Reggiano and the crispy sage leaves. Serve with the grilled bread generously doused in olive oil.

SERVES 4–6

SPICED LAMB & LENTIL SOUP

- 2 tablespoons extra-virgin olive oil
- 600 g lamb shoulder, cut into 8 cm pieces
- sea salt
- 1 onion, finely diced
- 1 celery stalk, finely diced
- 1 carrot, finely diced
- 2 garlic cloves, crushed with the side of the knife
- 1 teaspoon ground ginger
- 1 teaspoon cumin seeds, toasted
- 1 teaspoon ground coriander
- ½ teaspoon ground turmeric
- 1 cinnamon stick
- 400 g can crushed tomatoes
- 2 litres chicken or vegetable stock
- pinch of saffron threads
- 250 g puy lentils, rinsed
- 400 g can chickpeas, drained and rinsed
- large handful of coriander leaves, finely chopped
- large handful of parsley leaves, finely chopped
- black pepper

TO SERVE

- lemon wedges
- full-fat Greek yoghurt

This fragrant soup of lamb, spices and lentils is very much inspired by Moroccan harira, which is the general term for a soup filled with chickpeas, lentils or beans. Often with broken vermicelli included, it is a hearty and nourishing dish traditionally eaten to break the fast during Ramadan. Claudia Roden writes in her book *A New Book of Middle Eastern Food*: 'During the thirty days of the fast of Ramadan, every household prepares its own version of this national soup. The smell permeates the streets of Morocco, long before sunset, when it's time to break the fast.' This soup is wonderful, if not better, made ahead of time.

Heat the olive oil in a large saucepan over a medium–high heat. Season the lamb with salt, add to the pan and cook for 3–4 minutes or until browned on all sides. Remove the lamb from the pan and set aside. Drain all but 1 tablespoon of oil from the pan.

Reduce the heat to medium–low, add the onion, celery and carrot to the pan and cook for 8–10 minutes or until the vegetables are softened and beginning to colour. Add the garlic and spices and cook, stirring frequently, for 1 minute or until fragrant.

Return the lamb to the pan and add the tomatoes, stock and saffron. Increase the heat to medium–high and bring to a simmer. Once simmering, reduce the heat back to medium–low, cover and cook for 1½ hours or until the lamb is tender.

Add the lentils to the pan and cook for 25–30 minutes or until they are tender. Add the chickpeas and cook for a further 10 minutes. Stir through most of the herbs, reserving some to serve, and check for seasoning, adding salt and pepper to taste.

Serve the soup with plenty of lemon wedges, the remaining herbs and a dollop of yoghurt.

SERVES 6

CHAPTER THREE

Pasta, rice & gnocchi

PAGES 66–99

Perfectly ripe tomatoes, squishy from the hot sun, become a simple summery pasta.

STRACCI

WITH ZUCCHINI & THEIR FLOWERS

Stracci, also known as stracce and sagne stracce, literally means 'rags' and is found across many regions in Italy, such as Liguria, Tuscany, Lazio and the Marche. In *Encyclopedia of Pasta*, Oretta Zanini De Vita describes a sauce perfect for sagne stracci – onion, tomato, chilli, sometimes pork and lots of local pecorino. It's a great pasta shape to serve with the melty red onion and pork sausage sauce on page 86 and also the lamb ragù on page 92. While stracci is the perfect vehicle for a meaty tomato sauce, I also love it in early summer with young zucchini and their flowers. A little crème fraîche and some pecorino, and it is a pure treat. Use dried stracci or another pasta of your choice if you don't want to make the pasta.

I like to use a puntarelle cutter here – something, as the name suggests, designed to cut the Italian chicory puntarelle. It juliennes the zucchini perfectly and very quickly. You can simply use a knife to hand cut them if you don't have one.

- 3 tablespoons extra-virgin olive oil
- 2 garlic cloves, left whole and unpeeled
- 1 dried red chilli
- 500 g young small zucchini, julienned using a puntarelle cutter or a knife
- 2–3 tablespoons crème fraîche
- 1 tablespoon unsalted butter
- small handful of basil leaves
- 20 g Pecorino Romano, grated, plus extra to serve
- 6 male zucchini flowers, stamens removed, torn
- finely grated zest of 1 lemon
- sea salt and black pepper

PASTA DOUGH

- 400 g tipo 00 flour
- good pinch of sea salt
- 4 eggs
- semolina flour (semola rimacinata), for dusting

To make the pasta dough, tip the flour and salt onto a clean work surface and mix to combine. Create a well in the centre and crack in the eggs. Gently whisk the eggs with a fork, then slowly bring in the flour and mix to incorporate. When the dough becomes stiff, use your hands to mix until the dough has mostly come together. Knead for 10 minutes or until the dough is smooth and elastic. Cover with an upturned bowl and rest at room temperature for at least 30 minutes.

Divide the dough into four equal portions. On a lightly floured work surface and working with one piece at a time (cover the remaining dough with the upturned bowl), roll the dough into a rough disc around 1 cm thick. Roll the dough through a pasta machine through the widest few settings. Fold the dough into the centre from both of the shortest sides, like you're closing a book, then rotate it 90 degrees. Repeat this a few times through the first few settings to encourage the pasta to form a sheet and help make the pasta strong.

Now roll the dough continuously through the settings until the pasta is around 1 mm thick. Repeat with the remaining pieces of dough.

Using a fluted pasta cutter, cut the pasta dough into rough 4 cm diamonds or squares. Dust with the semolina flour and set aside on a tea towel dusted with semolina flour.

Warm the olive oil in a large frying pan over a medium heat, add the garlic and chilli and fry until aromatic, then remove from the oil using a slotted spoon. Add the zucchini and cook for 6–8 minutes or until softened a little.

Cook the pasta in a large saucepan of salted boiling water until just before al dente, 1–2 minutes.

While the pasta is cooking, add the crème fraîche, butter, basil and a ladleful of pasta cooking water to the zucchini. Transfer the pasta directly to the pan with a slotted spoon or sieve, add the Pecorino Romano, zucchini flowers, lemon zest and more pasta cooking water, if needed. Toss to create a luscious sauce. Season to taste and serve with more grated Pecorino Romano.

SERVES 4

SPINACH RICOTTA GNOCCHI

WITH CREAM & NUTMEG

These spinach ricotta gnocchi are simple to make, elegant and light. I love serving small portions as an entrée if I have friends over, but they are equally as satisfying eaten in mounds on a weeknight topped with a healthy amount of grated Parmigiano Reggiano. If you don't have a blender or food processor, you can simply finely chop the spinach and then combine everything in a bowl before adding in the flour and mixing. This is a more traditional way and will result in a mottled green dough that is just as delicious. Sometimes I serve these gnocchi with a simple sauce made from cherry tomatoes and garlic instead.

- 1 bunch of English spinach (around 150 g), large stems discarded
- 2 egg yolks
- 300 g fresh full-fat ricotta, drained
- pinch of freshly grated nutmeg
- 45 g Parmigiano Reggiano, grated, plus extra to serve
- sea salt and black pepper
- 75–100 g tipo 00 flour, plus extra for dusting

CREAM SAUCE

- 2 tablespoons unsalted butter
- small handful of sage leaves
- 200 ml pure cream
- good grating of fresh nutmeg
- sea salt and black pepper

Blanch the spinach in a large saucepan of salted boiling water until vibrant and just cooked, around 2 minutes. Drain and, when cool enough to touch, squeeze out as much liquid as possible. Transfer to a high-speed blender or food processor, add the egg yolks and ricotta and blitz to a fairly smooth consistency. Transfer to a bowl, along with the nutmeg and Parmigiano Reggiano. Mix well and season to taste. Add just enough flour to create a soft and slightly sticky dough. The less flour you add, the lighter the gnocchi will be.

Dust your work surface with a good amount of flour, drop a tablespoon of dough into the flour and turn to coat, then roll into a ball and set aside on a tray lined with baking paper. Repeat until all the dough is used. Refrigerate for 30 minutes.

To make the cream sauce, warm the butter in a frying pan over a medium heat and add the sage. Cook for 1 minute to infuse the butter with the sage, then add the cream and nutmeg. Season to taste, then cook for 2–3 minutes or until the sauce has reduced a little.

Meanwhile, cook the gnocchi in batches in a large saucepan of salted boiling water. Once they rise to the surface, continue to cook for 1–2 minutes more or until cooked through.

Use a slotted spoon to transfer the gnocchi to the sauce, then gently toss to coat. Add a splash of the cooking water to the pan to help create a looser sauce, if needed. Transfer the gnocchi to a serving plate, top with plenty of extra grated Parmigiano Reggiano and serve.

SERVES 4

RED PEPPER TORTIGLIONI

Tortiglioni is one of my favourite pasta shapes. Not dissimilar to rigatoni (another favourite), its ridges twirl around the hollow tube instead of straight up and down. It's a great sauce catcher and I simply love the name – it comes from the Vulgar Latin verb 'tortillare', which means to twist. I really love pasta corta (short pasta) with this sweet and slightly spicy sauce, but whatever shape you prefer will be fine. Don't hurry the cooking of the capsicums – it is important that they are cooked until they are very soft to ensure the right texture and sweetness.

- 3 tablespoons extra-virgin olive oil
- pinch of chilli flakes
- 2 red capsicums (around 400 g), sliced into 8 mm thick lengths
- 3 garlic cloves, crushed with the side of a knife
- 400 g can whole peeled tomatoes
- small handful of basil leaves
- 380 g tortiglioni
- sea salt and black pepper
- Parmigiano Reggiano or ricotta salata, grated, to serve

Warm the olive oil, chilli flakes and capsicum in a large frying pan over a low heat. Cook until the capsicum is very soft, around 20 minutes. Add the garlic and cook for 1–2 minutes or until aromatic. Add the tomatoes, breaking them up with the back of a wooden spoon, 100 ml of water and the basil and gently simmer for 15–20 minutes or until the sauce is thick and luscious.

Cook the tortiglioni in a large saucepan of salted boiling water until just before al dente. Transfer the pasta directly to the sauce using a slotted spoon or sieve. Add around a ladleful of pasta cooking water, as needed, to the sauce, to ensure the sauce beautifully coats the pasta. Cook the pasta in the sauce, giving it an occasional stir, until al dente. Season to taste and serve with a scattering of cheese.

SERVES 4

RISI E BISI

Risi e bisi translates to 'rice and peas' in the Venetian dialect. It is not a risotto, but a slightly looser rice dish that is eaten with a spoon. Traditionally, it was made to celebrate new spring peas, but frozen are more than fine. You will just need to make or buy a vegetable stock to use. I do like to use fresh peas, more for the stock made with the pea pods than anything else. I don't believe a good risi e bisi needs to be stirred constantly or have liquid added incrementally, like a risotto, but the occasional nudge with a wooden spoon does produce a creamier result. Vialone Nano is the preferred rice for this dish, as it tends to be starchier than other risotto rices and absorbs the broth really nicely.

- 600 g fresh peas in their pods or 300 g shelled or frozen peas
- sea salt
- 1.5 litres light vegetable stock (if using already podded or frozen peas)
- 60 g flat pancetta, cut into lardons
- 2 tablespoons extra-virgin olive oil, plus extra for drizzling
- 2 tablespoons unsalted butter
- 3 shallots, finely diced
- 250 g Vialone Nano rice or other risotto rice
- large handful of parsley leaves, finely chopped
- 60 g Parmigiano Reggiano, grated
- black pepper

If using peas in their pods, shell the peas and set them aside. Place half the pods in a large saucepan (discard the remaining pods). Cover with 3 litres of water, season with salt and place over a medium–high heat. Simmer for 45 minutes, then strain the stock into another saucepan and keep warm. If using frozen peas, warm the vegetable stock in a saucepan.

Place the pancetta in a large saucepan and cook over a medium–low heat for 6–8 minutes or until beginning to colour and most of the fat has rendered out. Remove the pancetta with a slotted spoon, leaving the oil in the pan. Add the olive oil and half the butter, along with the shallot. Reduce the heat to low and gently cook, stirring occasionally, for 6–8 minutes or until the shallot is softened. Add the rice and stir to coat. Pour in 1 litre of the warm stock and stir well. Gently cook the rice for 10 minutes, stirring often.

Add the peas to the pan and continue to cook for 5 minutes or until the rice is al dente. In the final minutes, return the pancetta to the rice, stir through the parsley, the remaining butter and the Parmigiano Reggiano and mix well to incorporate. If the rice dries out during cooking, add more stock or water, as needed. The finished consistency should be looser than a risotto but thicker than a soup. Season to taste, then serve with a drizzle of extra olive oil.

SERVES 4

MEZZI RIGATONI

WITH BROCCOLI, ALMONDS, MINT & ANCHOVIES

A classic pasta for winter that makes use of plenty of broccoli and a whole bunch of pantry staples. The anchovies add a salty depth to this dish, but you can absolutely leave them out to make this vegetarian if necessary. While this would often be served with orecchiette in Puglia, I also love it with mezzi rigatoni. The almonds in the breadcrumbs and the addition of mint are a little twist on a much-loved favourite. If you see it in the greengrocer or at the market, romanesco broccoli is great here, too.

- 800 g broccoli (2 large heads), broken into florets, stalks trimmed and roughly chopped
- 3 tablespoons extra-virgin olive oil, plus extra for drizzling
- 3 garlic cloves, finely sliced
- ½ teaspoon chilli flakes, plus extra to serve
- 8 anchovy fillets in olive oil, drained
- black pepper
- 380 g mezzi rigatoni
- finely grated zest and juice of 1 lemon

ALMOND BREADCRUMBS

- 2 tablespoons extra-virgin olive oil
- 60 g almonds, roughly chopped
- 40 g fresh breadcrumbs
- pinch of sea salt

Cook the broccoli in a large saucepan of salted boiling water until tender. Remove the broccoli with a slotted spoon or sieve and set aside, reserving the boiling water in the pan for the pasta.

For the almond breadcrumbs, warm the olive oil in a frying pan over a medium heat. Add the almonds and breadcrumbs and cook for 3–4 minutes or until golden. Transfer to a bowl and season with salt.

Warm the olive oil in a large frying pan over a medium–low heat and add the garlic, chilli flakes and anchovies. Cook for 1–2 minutes or until the garlic is aromatic and the anchovies have mostly dissolved in the oil. Add the broccoli along with a ladleful of the cooking water and cook, breaking up the broccoli with a wooden spoon and adding more water as needed, for 6–8 minutes or until the broccoli is very soft, but still vibrant. Season to taste.

Cook the pasta in the pan of reserved salted boiling water until just before al dente. Use a slotted spoon or sieve to scoop out the pasta and transfer it directly to the broccoli. Add the lemon zest and juice, plus more pasta cooking water if needed. Continue cooking the pasta in the sauce, giving it an occasional stir, until al dente.

Serve the broccoli and pasta topped with the almond breadcrumbs and a drizzle of extra olive oil.

SERVES 4

SPAGHETTI ALLA CARRETTIERA

When tomatoes are at their best, it usually means it's far too hot to be in the kitchen cooking all day. The answer is this fresh tomato pasta that should only be made with the best and ripest tomatoes. According to Mary Taylor Simeti in her book *Sicilian Food*, the dish is named after cart drivers. Simple and quick, it could be made on the roadside while their pasta cooked over a campfire. Served with plenty of ricotta salata, this is one of the most special ways to use beautiful tomatoes.

- 5 very ripe tomatoes (around 700 g)
- 2 garlic cloves
- sea salt
- large handful of basil leaves, plus extra to serve
- pinch of chilli flakes
- 3 tablespoons extra-virgin olive oil, plus extra for drizzling
- 400 g spaghetti
- ricotta salata, grated, to serve

Make a shallow cross with a sharp knife in the base of the tomatoes. Blanch for just a minute in a large saucepan of boiling water. Transfer with a slotted spoon to an ice bath. Peel the tomatoes, remove the core, and roughly chop. Transfer to a bowl, along with the juices, and set aside.

Pound the garlic and a pinch of salt to a fine paste using a mortar and pestle. Add the basil and chilli flakes and continue to pound until fairly smooth. Add the chopped tomato and all the juices and pound briefly to break the tomato down just a little into a rough sauce. Pour in the olive oil, season to taste with salt and allow to sit at room temperature for at least 30 minutes, but ideally a few hours.

Cook the spaghetti in a large saucepan of salted boiling water until al dente.

While the pasta is cooking, spoon half the sauce into a large serving bowl. Drain the cooked spaghetti or use tongs to transfer it directly to the sauce; stir to coat. Continue adding the remaining sauce until you have the desired amount. Any leftover sauce can be used for bruschetta.

Drizzle extra olive oil over the pasta, then scatter on the extra basil leaves and a generous grating of ricotta salata.

SERVES 4–6

BROTHY SEAFOOD RICE

- 3 tablespoons extra-virgin olive oil, plus extra for drizzling
- 4 shallots, finely diced
- 3 garlic cloves, roughly chopped
- large handful of coriander, roots and stems finely chopped, leaves roughly chopped
- 250 g Spanish bomba rice
- 2 teaspoons sweet smoked paprika
- 150 ml dry white wine
- 4 tomatoes, peeled, cored and roughly chopped
- pinch of saffron threads
- 500 g clams
- 500 g mussels, scrubbed and debearded
- 300 g skinless firm white fish fillets (such as snapper), cut into 4 cm pieces
- sea salt and black pepper

PRAWN HEAD STOCK

- 1 tablespoon extra-virgin olive oil
- 8 raw king prawns (approximately 700 g), peeled and deveined with tails intact, heads and shells reserved
- 1 litre fish stock

TO SERVE

- 1 long red chilli, finely chopped (optional)
- lemon wedges

This recipe is inspired by the classic Portuguese dish arroz de marisco. Loaded with beautiful seafood and flavoured with paprika, coriander and saffron, it's a comforting meal that relies on the quality of your seafood. Here, I use clams, mussels, prawns and fish for a seafood feast and utilise the prawn heads to enrich the fish stock. The extra effort is well worth it.

Traditionally made with Portuguese Carolino rice, I've suggested Spanish bomba rice instead, which is far easier to find. Alternatively, a risotto rice such as Carnaroli, Vialone Nano or arborio will be fine.

For the prawn head stock, heat the olive oil in a large saucepan over a medium–high heat and add the reserved prawn heads and shells (keep the prawns for the rice). Cook for 3–4 minutes, breaking the shells up as much as possible with the back of a wooden spoon. Pour in the stock and 1 litre of water and bring to a simmer. Cook for 30 minutes, then strain the stock into another saucepan and keep warm.

Warm the olive oil in a large saucepan over a medium–low heat, add the shallot, garlic and finely chopped coriander roots and stems and cook for 8–10 minutes or until the shallot and garlic are softened and beginning to colour. Increase the heat to medium and scatter in the rice. Cook for 1–2 minutes to toast the grains, then add the paprika and cook for 30 seconds. Pour in the wine and simmer, stirring often, for 2–3 minutes until reduced. Add the tomato and cook for another 3–4 minutes or until the tomato has collapsed into the rice. Add 1.5 litres of the warm prawn head stock and the saffron and simmer for 15 minutes or until the rice is almost al dente but still a little undercooked. The rice should be quite brothy, so add any of the remaining stock, or simply water, as needed to the pan at any point.

Add the clams and mussels to the pan and cover with a lid. Cook for 3–4 minutes or until they open. Add the reserved prawns and fish and cook for a further 2–3 minutes or until they are just cooked. Season to taste and stir through the chopped coriander leaves.

Serve the brothy rice topped with the chilli, if using, lemon wedges and a drizzle of extra olive oil.

SERVES 4–6

BIGOLI IN SALSA

I first ate this inimitable pasta in a tiny osteria in Verona. The winding wooden stairs led us up to a very small dining room. The wholewheat bigoli were chewy and thick and smothered in the most delicious sauce of slow-cooked onions and anchovies – bigoli in salsa. Following that lunch, bigoli in salsa became my staple at home whenever I had a bare fridge or was not sure what to cook. Fresh bigoli, traditionally made by extruding the dough through a hand-cranked machine called a bigolaro, is near impossible to find outside of the Veneto region. However, dried bigoli is more readily available and, if not, simply use spaghetti or even bucatini. The amount of anchovies may seem excessive, but they cook down to become a rich saltiness that carries the dish so nicely.

- 3 tablespoons extra-virgin olive oil
- 2 onions, halved and finely sliced
- sea salt
- 12 anchovy fillets
- 3 tablespoons dry white wine
- 380 g bigoli or other pasta of your choice
- large handful of parsley leaves, finely chopped
- black pepper

Warm the olive oil in a large frying pan over a low heat, add the onion and a pinch of salt and gently cook for 12–15 minutes or until the onion is softened and just beginning to colour. Stir occasionally to avoid burning.

Meanwhile, prepare the anchovies by either rinsing them if packed in salt or, if in olive oil, simply draining them. Add the anchovies to the pan, breaking them up with the back of a wooden spoon. When mostly dissolved, increase the heat to medium and deglaze with the wine, scraping the bottom of the pan to lift any brown bits and allowing it to simmer for a minute. Remove from the heat and keep warm.

Meanwhile, cook the bigoli in salted boiling water until just before al dente. Drain the pasta, reserving 125 ml (½ cup) of the pasta cooking water.

Place the pan with the onion and anchovies over a medium heat. Add the cooked pasta and about half the reserved pasta cooking water. Stir to coat the pasta in the sauce and finish cooking the bigoli until al dente, adding more reserved pasta cooking water, if needed, to loosen the sauce. Stir in the parsley, season to taste and serve.

SERVES 4

LUMACHE

WITH MELTY RED ONION & SAUSAGE

When I lived in Tuscany, I learned that one should not automatically use garlic and onion together. They each have a purpose and should be used thoughtfully and often singularly. A similar lesson on the automatic use of salt and pepper was also had. Sometimes I still revert to using both, when I think it's beneficial or necessary, but those learnings made me rethink everything I knew about cooking and especially making pasta sauces. Here onions are the hero and needn't be overshadowed by garlic in any sense. They are cooked down for almost half an hour until very soft and 'melty'. The result is a sweet and fragrant sauce, spiked with herbs and enriched by the sausage meat. It is a simple sauce that requires only humble ingredients and some time.

- 1 tablespoon extra-virgin olive oil
- 4 pork and fennel sausages, casings removed
- 3 large red onions, finely sliced
- sea salt
- 2 tablespoons tomato paste
- 100 ml dry white wine
- 400 g can whole peeled tomatoes
- 4 sage leaves
- 2 oregano sprigs
- black pepper
- 380 g lumache or other pasta of your choice
- grated Parmigiano Reggiano, to serve

Warm the olive oil in a large frying pan over a medium–high heat, then drop tablespoon-sized balls of the sausage meat into the pan and fry until golden on all sides. Remove the meatballs with a slotted spoon.

Reduce the heat to low, add the onion and a pinch of salt to the pan and gently fry for 20–25 minutes or until the onion is very soft and beginning to caramelise. Stir often to prevent the onion from burning. Add the tomato paste and fry off for 1–2 minutes, then deglaze with the wine, scraping the bottom of the pan to lift any brown bits, and simmer for 1–2 minutes until slightly reduced. Add the tomatoes, 400 ml of water and the sage and oregano. Return the meatballs to the pan and stir to coat in the sauce. Gently simmer for 30–35 minutes or until the sauce is thick and rich. Season to taste and keep warm.

Cook the lumache in a large saucepan of salted boiling water until just before al dente. Using a slotted spoon or sieve, transfer the pasta directly to the sauce and increase the heat to medium–high. Toss the pasta through the sauce, adding some of the pasta cooking water, as needed. Continue cooking until the pasta is al dente. Season to taste and serve with plenty of Parmigiano Reggiano.

SERVES 4

LIGURIAN FISH RAVIOLI

WITH TOMATO & PRAWNS

Inspired by zembi d'arzillo from the Ligurian coast, this delicate yet utterly delicious pasta is one of my favourite things to make when I really want to go all out. Not only am I making fresh pasta but I'm filling it with fish and serving it with prawns.

I first came across this dish in *The Mediterranean Kitchen* written by influential American chef, Joyce Goldstein. My version is rather different but the essence of it remains. It's luxurious yet still simple and always so well loved when I cook it.

Traditionally, zembi d'arzillo is served with either a simple tomato sauce or one of limpets or clams and tomatoes, though I love to make it with prawns – roughly chopped so every mouthful of ravioli is joined by some prawns.

The etymology of zembi d'arzillo is truly fascinating. The word 'zembi' has Arabic roots, coming from the word 'zembil' – a woven basket used for transportation by fishermen – and 'arzillo' is the name of the evocative scent of the sea, specifically from the seaweed around the rocks. It is a recipe very much of the place and its history.

PASTA DOUGH

- 300 g tipo 00 flour
- pinch of sea salt
- 3 eggs
- semolina flour (semola rimacinata), for dusting

FISH FILLING

- 2 tablespoons extra-virgin olive oil
- 500 g skinless snapper fillets, pin-boned
- 2 marjoram sprigs, leaves picked
- sea salt
- finely grated zest of 1 lemon
- 1 garlic clove, finely grated
- 40 g Parmigiano Reggiano, grated
- 1 egg, lightly whisked

PRAWN AND TOMATO SAUCE

- 2 tablespoons extra-virgin olive oil, plus extra for drizzling
- 1 garlic clove, crushed with the side of a knife
- 300 g cherry tomatoes
- 300 g prawn meat, roughly chopped
- 3 tablespoons prosecco or white wine
- 2 tablespoons unsalted butter
- handful of parsley leaves, roughly chopped
- sea salt

For the pasta dough, tip the flour and salt onto a clean work surface and mix to combine. Create a well in the centre and crack in the eggs. Gently whisk the eggs with a fork, then slowly bring in the flour and mix to incorporate. When the dough becomes stiff, use your hands to finish bringing the dough together. Knead for 10 minutes or until the dough is smooth and elastic. You want to knead with a rocking motion, pushing the dough away from you, then bringing it back to the middle, rotating it 90 degrees, then repeating. This encourages a smooth surface and a nice round shape. Cover with an upturned bowl and rest at room temperature for at least 30 minutes.

For the fish filling, heat the olive oil in a frying pan and add the fish and marjoram. Season with a little salt, then cook for 2–3 minutes on each side or until the fish is just cooked. Transfer to a bowl and add the lemon zest, garlic, Parmigiano Reggiano and egg. Mix to combine and season to taste with salt. Set aside.

Take one third of the dough and, on a lightly floured work surface and working with one piece at a time (cover the remaining dough again with the upturned bowl), roll the dough into a rough disc around 1 cm thick. Roll the dough through a pasta machine through the widest few settings. Fold the dough into the centre from both of the shortest sides, like you're closing a book, then rotate it 90 degrees. Move to the next setting, folding and rolling. Repeat this a few times through the first few settings to encourage the pasta to form a sheet and help make the pasta strong. Now roll the dough continuously through the settings until the pasta is around 0.8 mm thick.

Place tablespoon amounts of the fish filling along one long edge of the pasta sheet, leaving a 1 cm border at the edge and around 2.5 cm of space between each mound of filling. Fold the empty side of the pasta sheet over the filling to meet the other pasta edge and press and seal around each mound of filling to remove any excess air. Press down and seal along the edge of the pasta sheet, dabbing with a little water if necessary to help the pasta stick. Use a fluted pasta cutter to cut along the length of the sheet, being careful not to trim too close to the filling. Finish by cutting in between each mound to give you the ravioli. Set aside on a tea towel lightly dusted with semolina flour.

Repeat with the remaining dough and filling.

For the prawn and tomato sauce, heat the olive oil in a frying pan over a medium heat. Add the garlic and cook for 1–2 minutes or until aromatic. Remove the garlic from the oil with a slotted spoon. Tip the tomatoes into the pan and cook for 3–4 minutes or until just beginning to collapse. Add the prawn meat, stir to coat, then add the prosecco or wine and reduce a little for 1–2 minutes. If the sauce dries out too much, simply add some of the pasta cooking water. Add the butter and stir to thicken. Stir through some parsley and season to taste.

Meanwhile, cook the ravioli, in batches if needed, in salted boiling water for 3–4 minutes or until al dente. Transfer the ravioli to a serving plate and spoon on the sauce. Drizzle with some extra olive oil and serve.

SERVES 4

Recipe images overleaf

UMBRICELLI

WITH LAMB RAGÙ

Hailing from Umbria, umbricelli is a thick hand-rolled spaghetti also known as strangozzi or pici or lunghetti in Tuscany. Here, made without eggs, this soft dough is transformed into long worm-like shapes – perfect for a hearty lamb ragù. It's a great pasta to make if you've never attempted fresh pasta before as it requires simply flour and water and no special equipment. The lamb ragù is rich and unctuous and benefits from low and slow cooking. This is something I like to make on a Sunday morning when everyone is pottering around the house and I am not in a hurry. Something like this simply cannot be rushed.

- 3 tablespoons extra-virgin olive oil, plus extra for drizzling
- 800 g lamb shoulder, cut into 8 cm pieces
- sea salt
- 1 onion, finely diced
- 1 carrot, finely diced
- 2 celery stalks, finely diced
- 3 garlic cloves, roughly chopped
- 2 rosemary sprigs
- pinch of chilli flakes
- 150 ml dry white wine
- 800 g canned tomato polpa (finely crushed tomatoes)
- 250 ml (1 cup) chicken stock
- black pepper
- grated Pecorino Romano, to serve

PASTA DOUGH

- 400 g tipo 00 flour
- pinch of sea salt
- 200 ml warm water
- semolina flour (semola rimacinata), for dusting

Heat 1 tablespoon of the olive oil in a large saucepan over a medium–high heat. Season the lamb with salt, then cook for 4–5 minutes until browned well on all sides. Remove the lamb from the pan and drain off all the fat.

Warm the remaining 2 tablespoons of olive oil in the same pan over a medium–low heat. Add the onion, carrot, celery and a pinch of salt and cook, stirring occasionally, for 10–12 minutes until the vegetables are softened and beginning to colour. Add the garlic, rosemary and chilli flakes and cook for 2–3 minutes or until aromatic.

Increase the heat to medium–high, return the browned lamb to the pan and deglaze with the wine, scraping the bottom of the pan to lift any brown bits. Simmer for 1–2 minutes to slightly reduce the wine. Add the tomatoes and stock and bring to a simmer. Reduce the heat to low and cook, partially covered, for 3–3½ hours or until the lamb is tender and the sauce is thick and rich. If the meat is still in large pieces, use the wooden spoon to gently break it up into the sauce. Season to taste.

Meanwhile, to make the pasta dough, tip the flour and salt onto a clean work surface and mix to combine. Create a well in the centre, slowly pour in the water, then using your hands, slowly bring in the flour, a little at a time, and mix to incorporate. When the dough becomes stiff, really work hard to bring in as much of the flour as you can. A pastry scraper can help bring everything together. Knead for about 10 minutes or until the dough is smooth and elastic. Cover with an upturned bowl and rest at room temperature for at least 30 minutes.

Roll out the dough to form a disc around 1 cm thick, then drizzle with some olive oil to stop it from drying out. Cut the dough into 1 cm strips and roll each strip into a thin rope around 5 mm wide. Have a small bowl of water nearby in case the dough begins to dry out, so you can wet your fingertips to help keep the dough moist. Place the rolled umbricelli on a clean tea towel dusted with semolina flour.

Just before you cook the umbricelli, have the ragù heating over a medium heat.

Cook the umbricelli in a large saucepan of salted boiling water until chewy but not chalky, around 3–4 minutes. Drain the umbricelli, reserving some of the pasta cooking water. Add the umbricelli to the ragù along with as much cooking water as needed to help coat the pasta. Simmer the pasta and ragù for 1–2 minutes, until slightly thickened, then serve with plenty of grated Pecorino Romano.

SERVES 6

PASTA ALLA NORCINA

This elegant pasta is possibly my children's favourite dinner. I also love how comforting it is, while still being quick and totally achievable during the week. Hailing from Norcia, a walled town at the foothills of the Sibillini Mountains, this pasta is traditionally made with the iconic local Norcia sausage. Gently flavoured with garlic, white wine, salt, pepper and often nutmeg, I find the best substitute is a good-quality mild Italian-style pork sausage. The pasta water is especially important here to help create the silkiest sauce, which will envelop the pasta.

- 2 tablespoons extra-virgin olive oil
- 1 onion, finely diced
- sea salt
- 400 g Italian-style pork sausages, casings removed
- 125 ml (½ cup) dry white wine
- 200 ml pure cream
- generous pinch of freshly grated nutmeg
- black pepper
- 380 g rigatoni or paccheri rigati
- grated Pecorino Romano, to serve

Warm the olive oil in a large frying-pan over a medium–low heat. Add the onion and a pinch of salt and cook, stirring occasionally, for 8–10 minutes or until the onion is softened and just beginning to colour. Increase the heat to medium–high and add the sausage meat. Using the back of a wooden spoon, break the meat up into small pieces and cook for 3–4 minutes or until nicely coloured. Deglaze with the wine, scraping the bottom of the pan to lift any brown bits, and simmer for 2–3 minutes or until the liquid has reduced a little. Pour in the cream and stir to combine. Add the nutmeg, reduce the heat to medium–low and simmer for 8–10 minutes or until the sauce has thickened. Season to taste.

While the sauce is simmering, cook the pasta in a large saucepan of salted boiling water until just before al dente. Use a slotted spoon or sieve to scoop out the pasta and transfer it directly to the sauce; stir to coat. Add a ladleful of pasta cooking water and increase the heat to medium–high. Simmer for 2–3 minutes or until the pasta is al dente, adding more pasta water, as needed, to ensure the sauce stays nice and silky and doesn't dry out.

Serve with a generous grating of Pecorino Romano and freshly ground black pepper.

SERVES 4

LASAGNE

- 125 g flat pancetta, diced
- 1 onion, very finely diced
- 1 carrot, very finely diced
- 1 celery stalk, very finely diced
- sea salt
- 1–2 tablespoons extra-virgin olive oil, if needed
- 300 g pork mince
- 200 g beef mince
- 1 garlic clove, crushed with the side of a knife
- 1 rosemary sprig
- 1 fresh bay leaf
- 4 sage leaves
- 150 ml dry white wine
- 700 g tomato passata
- 500 ml (2 cups) chicken stock
- 2 cloves
- 150 g Parmigiano Reggiano, grated

SPINACH PASTA DOUGH

- 150 g English spinach leaves
- 3 eggs
- 400 g tipo 00 flour
- pinch of sea salt
- semolina flour (semola rimacinata), for dusting

BESCIAMELLA

- 1 litre full-cream milk
- 80 g unsalted butter, plus extra for greasing and dotting
- 80 g plain flour
- good pinch of freshly grated nutmeg
- sea salt and black pepper

Homemade lasagne is a labour of love, but what beautiful rewarding labour. It is what I make when I want to unwind and really sink into cooking for an afternoon. It is for Sundays when it's rainy outside, all the windows foggy from the kitchen warmth. Here the pasta dough is enriched with spinach for a vivid green that holds the rich ragù and besciamella. I buy the Parmigiano Reggiano already grated from my local deli. That is one kitchen task I don't particularly enjoy, especially when making lasagne. If you want to make regular pasta, simply use the ratio of 1 egg to 100 g of flour. The spinach in the dough makes the pasta a little more delicate to work with, so take care.

Place the pancetta in a large saucepan over a medium heat and cook for 3–4 minutes or until beginning to colour and the fat has rendered out. Add the onion, carrot, celery, a pinch of salt and some olive oil, if needed, and cook for 10–12 minutes or until the vegetables are soft and beginning to colour. Increase the heat to high, add the pork and beef minces, breaking the meat up with the back of a wooden spoon, and cook for 6–7 minutes or until browned. Add the garlic and herbs and stir well to combine. Deglaze with the wine, scraping the bottom of the pan to lift any brown bits, and simmer for 1–2 minutes to let the alcohol evaporate. Add the tomato passata, stock and cloves and bring to the boil. Reduce the heat to low and cook, covered, for 1½–2 hours or until the ragù is thick and rich. If the ragù becomes too dry during cooking, a little water can be added.

For the spinach pasta dough, blanch the spinach in salted boiling water, then drain, refresh in iced water and drain again. Place in a food processor with the eggs and blitz until smooth. Alternatively, finely chop the blanched spinach and mix with the eggs in a small bowl. Tip the flour and salt onto a clean work surface and combine with your hands. Create a well in the centre, pour in the spinach mixture and gently whisk with a fork. Slowly bring in the flour and mix to incorporate. When the dough becomes stiff, use your hands to finish bringing the dough together. Knead for 10 minutes or until the dough is smooth and elastic. You want to knead with a rocking motion, pushing the dough away from you, then bringing it back to the middle, rotating it 90 degrees, then repeating. This encourages a smooth surface and a nice round shape. Cover with an upturned bowl and rest at room temperature for at least 30 minutes.

On a lightly floured work surface, roll one-quarter of the dough into a rough disc around 1 cm thick. (Cover the remaining dough with the upturned bowl.) Roll the dough through a pasta machine through the widest few settings. Fold the dough into the centre from both of the shortest sides, like you're closing a book, then rotate it 90 degrees. Repeat this a few times through the first few settings to encourage the pasta to form a sheet and help make the pasta strong. Now roll the dough continuously through the settings until the pasta is around 0.8–1 mm thick. Repeat with the remaining dough. Cut the pasta sheets into 30 cm lengths and dust with semolina flour, if needed.

Blanch the pasta sheets, a few at a time, in plenty of salted boiling water for 1 minute. Refresh in a bowl of iced water, then place them on clean tea towels. It is important that the cooked lasagne sheets do not touch each other as they will stick.

For the besciamella, warm the milk in a saucepan to just below simmering point; you don't want it to boil. In another saucepan, melt the butter over a medium heat and sprinkle in the flour. Whisk to form a roux and cook until the roux starts to colour, around 1–1½ minutes. Pour in the hot milk, whisking constantly to avoid any lumps. Reduce the heat to low and cook until the besciamella has thickened and coats the back of a wooden spoon, around 8–10 minutes. Stir in the nutmeg and season to taste.

Preheat the oven to 180°C fan-forced.

Grease a 30 cm square baking dish with butter and spread a small layer of ragù over the base. Add a pasta sheet, then a more generous spoonful of ragù. Top with some besciamella and a good scattering of Parmigiano. Continue until all the ingredients have been used, finishing with a layer of pasta, ragù, besciamella and plenty of Parmigiano. In this size dish, you will have six to seven layers. A larger dish will produce a shorter lasagne.

Dot the top of the lasagne with some extra butter and bake for 35–40 minutes or until golden and bubbling. Allow to sit for at least 10 minutes before serving.

SERVES 8–10

Recipe images overleaf

CHAPTER FOUR

Substantial plates for the table

PAGES 100–141

Most meals
I enjoy have
two things
in common:
good-quality
seasonal
produce and
simple cooking.

STUFFED SARDINES

WITH BREADCRUMBS, PINE NUTS & CURRANTS

These stuffed sardines, or sarde a beccafico, are an incredibly well-loved Sicilian constant. They are a wonderful example of cucina povera. Initially created to imitate a luxurious delicacy of beccafico (which means 'fig pecker' and refers to a prized songbird eaten by nobles), these stuffed sardines – said to look like the small birds once rolled – were far more economical. Plainly speaking, this dish is a gorgeous celebration of sardines stuffed with strong Sicilian flavours.

- 2 tablespoons extra-virgin olive oil, plus extra for greasing
- 500 g butterflied sardine fillets
- sea salt

FILLING

- 30 g currants
- finely grated zest and juice of ½ orange
- 80 g fresh breadcrumbs
- large handful of mint leaves, finely chopped
- large handful of parsley leaves, finely chopped
- 2 anchovy fillets, finely chopped
- 30 g pine nuts, toasted
- 2 teaspoons red wine vinegar
- sea salt and black pepper

Preheat the oven to 180°C fan-forced. Grease a 28 cm round baking dish with some olive oil and set aside.

For the filling, place the currants and orange zest and juice in a bowl and allow to soak for 10 minutes. Add the breadcrumbs, herbs, anchovies, pine nuts and vinegar and season to taste. Set aside 1 tablespoon of the filling for serving.

Working with one sardine at a time, place the sardine, skin-side down, on a clean work surface, then spoon 1 heaped teaspoon of the filling into the centre of the fillet and roll up. Place in the dish, seam-side down. Repeat with the remaining fillets and filling, arranging the stuffed sardines in a circular fashion in the dish. Scatter over the reserved filling, drizzle on the olive oil and season with a little salt.

Bake the sardines for 20 minutes or until they are cooked through and the breadcrumbs are crunchy.

SERVES 4

CRUMBED FISH

WITH YOGHURT TARTARE & SOFT POTATO BUNS

The joyful reward of making these buns from scratch is something very special. You can definitely use store-bought buns for these fish burgers, but if you feel like a little project and want to make them, the effort is very much worth it. They're soft, squishy and an unmatched choice to hold the crunchy crumbed fish and voluptuous yoghurt tartare. The secret to these buns' texture is the potato, but also the tangzhong, which is flour and water or milk cooked into a roux and then added to the dough as a dough improver. It is a technique that has been used for centuries in Chinese cooking and is similar to the Japanese method called yudane.

1 egg, for egg wash

white and black sesame seeds, for sprinkling

neutral vegetable oil, for frying

iceberg lettuce leaves, shredded, to serve

8 slices of cheddar or American-style burger cheese

TANGZHONG

100 ml full-cream milk

25 g plain flour

MAIN DOUGH

1 potato (200 g), peeled, boiled and mashed

150 ml full-cream milk, warmed

500 g (3⅓ cups) plain flour

10 g active dried yeast

5 g fine sea salt

25 g caster sugar

1 egg

40 g unsalted butter, softened, plus extra for greasing

2 tablespoons neutral vegetable oil

For the tangzhong, combine the milk and flour in a small saucepan over a medium heat. Mix constantly to avoid lumps and cook for 2–3 minutes or until gel-like in consistency. Set aside to cool. Place the tangzhong in the large bowl of a stand mixer fitted with the dough hook attachment and add the main dough ingredients. Mix for 2–3 minutes on a medium–low speed to combine, then mix on a medium speed for 15–18 minutes or until the dough is smooth, elastic and strong. To check whether enough gluten has developed in the dough, stop the mixer and pull out a little piece of the dough. With both your hands, stretch it out. It should stretch without tearing until almost transparent. This is called the 'windowpane method'. Continue mixing and checking until you can create the 'windowpane' successfully.

Transfer the dough to a lightly buttered large bowl. Cover with a damp tea towel and allow to rise in a warm spot for 1 hour or until doubled in size.

Divide the dough into eight balls, each approximately 130–140 g. Use your hands to shape them into smooth rounds and set on a baking tray, or divide between two trays. Be sure to leave some space between each bun as they will expand as they rise and bake. Cover loosely with a tea towel and allow to rise for 35–45 minutes or until light and puffy.

Preheat the oven to 195°C fan-forced.

Whisk the egg with 1 teaspoon of water in a small bowl, then brush the egg wash over the buns. Sprinkle on the sesame seeds and bake for 10–12 minutes or until the buns are golden and well risen. Set aside to cool.

YOGHURT TARTARE

- 150 g full-fat Greek yoghurt
- 80 g Japanese mayonnaise (or homemade, see page 177)
- 2 teaspoons dijon mustard
- finely grated zest of 1 lemon
- small handful of dill fronds, finely chopped
- small handful of parsley leaves, finely chopped
- 1 tablespoon salted capers, rinsed, drained and patted dry, roughly chopped
- 8 cornichons, finely chopped
- 1 shallot, finely chopped
- sea salt and black pepper

CRUMBED FLATHEAD

- 8 skinless flathead fillets, pin-boned
- sea salt and black pepper
- 1 egg
- 1 tablespoon full-cream milk
- plain flour, for dusting
- 100 g Japanese breadcrumbs (panko), for crumbing

Combine the yoghurt tartare ingredients in a bowl and place in the fridge until ready to serve.

For the crumbed flathead, season the fish with salt and pepper and set aside. Whisk the egg and milk in a shallow bowl. Sprinkle a layer of flour into another shallow bowl and place the breadcrumbs in a third shallow bowl. Working with one fillet at a time, and keeping one hand clean, dust the fish in the flour, shaking off any excess, then dip in the egg mix and finish with a coating of breadcrumbs, patting them on to ensure they stick. Transfer to a plate and continue with the remaining fillets.

Heat about 1 cm of vegetable oil in a large frying pan over a medium heat. Add the fish in batches and fry until golden and cooked through, around 2 minutes on each side. Drain on a wire rack and season with salt.

Split the buns in half and toast on a grill or in a frying pan, cut-side down, until lightly golden. Spoon a heaped tablespoon of yoghurt tartare onto the base of each bun. Top with some lettuce, a piece of fish, a slice of cheese and another dollop of the yoghurt tartare. Top with a bun lid and serve.

SERVES 8

Recipe images overleaf

FISH WRAPPED IN VINE LEAVES

WITH SALMORIGLIO

- 200 g vine leaves in brine, rinsed and dried
- 1 kg whole snapper, scaled and gutted
- 1 lemon, sliced
- 3 marjoram or oregano sprigs
- sea salt
- extra-virgin olive oil, for drizzling
- lemon wedges, to serve

SALMORIGLIO

- 2 garlic cloves, finely grated
- 3 oregano sprigs, leaves picked and finely chopped
- small handful of parsley leaves, finely chopped
- 1 tablespoon dried Sicilian or Greek oregano, crumbled
- finely grated zest of 1 lemon
- 80 ml (⅓ cup) lemon juice (from 2–3 lemons)
- 150 ml extra-virgin olive oil
- sea salt and black pepper

This is such a celebratory dish, one worthy of being in the centre of the table at a dinner party. It also happens to be a really simple way to cook fish and is perfect for a Sunday lunch or an al fresco dinner. I grew up eating whole fish, usually stuffed with Maltese flavours such as mint, tomato and capers. Here, I keep it incredibly pared back. The vine leaves are citrusy and tangy and help carry the lemon flavour through the fish. The salmoriglio, another lemony element, ties it all together for a light yet satisfying dish. My salmoriglio makes use of both dried and fresh oregano. It is a dressing or marinade from southern Italy and an absolute staple in my kitchen. I love it with grilled meats, vegetables and fish.

Combine the salmoriglio ingredients in a small bowl and mix well. Allow to sit at room temperature for 1–2 hours.

Preheat the oven to 180°C fan-forced. Line a baking tray with baking paper.

Place half the vine leaves on the tray, overlapping them slightly. Place the fish on the vine leaves, then add the lemon slices and marjoram or oregano to the cavity and season with salt. Drizzle the olive oil over the fish and season with salt. Cover the fish with the remaining vine leaves and bring up the overhanging vine leaves on the base to enclose the fish. Roast for 35 minutes or until the leaves are crispy and the fish is cooked through. Unwrap the fish at the table and serve with the salmoriglio and lemon wedges.

SERVES 4–6

KING GEORGE WHITING

WITH BRAISED PEAS & TARRAGON

A wonderful dish in spring, but frozen peas are also good here so you can make this year-round with ease. The pancetta adds a nice richness, but I have made it many times without, so omit if you prefer or don't have any on hand. Any fish of your choice that is suitable for pan-frying is great here. I like King George whiting but Murray cod, snapper and gurnard are all good choices.

- 1 tablespoon extra-virgin olive oil
- 3 tablespoons unsalted butter
- 4 × 150 g King George whiting fillets, skin on, pin-boned
- 100 ml dry white wine

BRAISED PEAS

- 100 g flat pancetta, cut into lardons
- 800 g fresh peas in their pods, shelled, or 400 g shelled fresh or frozen peas
- 250 ml (1 cup) chicken stock
- 1 garlic clove, crushed with the side of a knife
- large handful of tarragon leaves, finely chopped
- large handful of parsley leaves, finely chopped
- sea salt and black pepper

For the braised peas, place the pancetta in a large frying pan and set over a medium heat. Cook until the pancetta is beginning to colour and most of the fat has rendered out. Remove the pancetta with a slotted spoon and set aside. Add the peas, stock and garlic and bring to a simmer. Cook for 4–6 minutes or until the peas are tender and most of the liquid has reduced. Return the pancetta to the pan and warm through. Stir in the herbs, season to taste and keep warm.

Heat the olive oil and 1 tablespoon of the butter in a large frying pan over a medium–high heat. Add the fish, skin-side down, and cook for 2–3 minutes or until golden. Turn the fish over and pour the wine around the fish. Cook for 1 minute, then remove the fillets using a slotted spoon and keep warm. Add the remaining 2 tablespoons of butter and swirl in the pan to create a sauce. Cook the sauce for 1–2 minutes or until slightly reduced.

Spoon the peas onto a serving plate, top with the fish, skin-side up, and pour on the sauce. Serve.

SERVES 4

ONE-PAN CHICKEN

WITH OREGANO, ORANGE & GREEN OLIVES

One-pan chicken dinners are a saviour in the middle of the week when time is short and hunger levels are high. The combination of orange, oregano and green olives works so well and is the perfect balance of sweet, salty and herbaceous. Served with roast potatoes or simply some bread to mop up all the juices, this is a perennial favourite.

- 6 bone-in chicken thighs, skin on
- sea salt
- 2 tablespoons extra-virgin olive oil
- 100 ml dry white wine
- 150 ml chicken stock
- 6 shallots, quartered
- 3 garlic cloves, crushed with the side of a knife
- 3 oregano sprigs, plus extra to serve
- 1 orange, halved and sliced
- 100 g green Sicilian olives, pitted and roughly chopped

Preheat the oven to 180°C fan-forced.

Season the chicken with salt.

Heat the olive oil in a large ovenproof frying pan over a medium–high heat. Add the chicken, skin-side down, and cook for 3–4 minutes or until golden. Turn the chicken, then pour in the wine, being careful not to pour it directly over the chicken. Stir to deglaze, scraping the bottom of the pan to lift any brown bits. Simmer for 1–2 minutes or until reduced slightly. Add the stock and nestle the shallot, garlic, oregano and orange slices around the chicken. Transfer to the oven and bake for 30 minutes or until the chicken is cooked through and nicely coloured. Top with the olives and extra oregano, season to taste and serve.

SERVES 4–6

TARRAGON CHICKEN

I can count on one hand the dishes I ate growing up that weren't Maltese. This was one of them – a legacy from my mum's dinner party days of the 1970s. It's a classic, and for good reason. French tarragon is prized in my kitchen for its subtle aniseed flavour and sweetness – it also happens to be one of the herbs I grow successfully. If you don't want to use a whole chicken, the equivalent weight of skin-on bone-in chicken thighs works very well, too. I love to serve this simply with mashed or roast potatoes and some steamed spinach.

- 1 × 1.6–1.8 kg chicken, broken down into 6 pieces
- sea salt
- plain flour, for dusting
- 2 tablespoons extra-virgin olive oil
- 2 tablespoons unsalted butter
- 6 shallots, halved
- 125 ml (½ cup) dry white wine
- 250 ml (1 cup) pure cream
- 300 ml chicken stock
- handful of tarragon sprigs
- black pepper

Preheat the oven to 180°C fan-forced.

Season the chicken pieces with salt and dust in the flour, shaking off any excess.

Heat half the olive oil and butter in a large, deep ovenproof frying pan over a medium–high heat. When the butter is foaming, add the chicken, in batches if needed, and brown for 3 minutes on each side. Remove from the pan.

Wipe the pan clean and add the remaining olive oil and butter. Once the butter is foaming, add the shallot and a pinch of salt and cook for 4–5 minutes or until the shallot is beginning to colour. Deglaze with the wine, scraping the bottom of the pan to lift any brown bits. Cook for 1–2 minutes until reduced, then add the cream, stock and tarragon sprigs. Season with a little salt and pepper. Bring to a simmer and return the chicken, skin-side up, to the pan.

Transfer the pan to the oven and bake for 40–45 minutes or until the chicken is cooked through and the sauce has thickened. Check for seasoning, adding more salt and some black pepper if needed, then serve.

SERVES 4

ZA'ATAR CHICKEN

WITH YOGHURT & BUTTERY PINE NUTS

I first tried za'atar, the herb, here in Melbourne. My friend and chef, Tom Sarafian, first introduced me to it and whenever I see it at my local grocer, I always buy some. This wild herb, native to the Levant region, has a savoury and intense aroma with a complex flavour. Palestinian chef Sami Tamimi and co-author Tara Wigley describe the complexity in their book *Falastin* – 'there is a connection to oregano and marjoram but also to cumin, lemon, sage and mint'. Here, I use the za'atar spice mix, which is a combination of the dried za'atar herb, whole toasted sesame seeds, sumac and salt. It is such a versatile spice mix – wonderful with fish, served with flatbread and good olive oil or used in a marinade. The idea for pouring the hot buttery pine nuts over the cold yoghurt comes from the Egyptian and Levantine dish fatteh. The yoghurt must be very cold, so as you pour on the hot buttery pine nuts, you hear a 'tish' sound. This is a recipe I come back to over and over again.

- 4 chicken marylands (around 1.4 kg)
- 2 tablespoons za'atar spice mix
- 2 teaspoons ground cumin
- 1 teaspoon ground allspice
- 1 teaspoon sumac, plus extra to serve
- finely grated zest and juice of 1 lemon
- 2 garlic cloves, grated
- 2 tablespoons extra-virgin olive oil, plus extra for drizzling
- sea salt and black pepper
- 4 potatoes, peeled and cut into chips
- 400 g can whole peeled tomatoes, drained
- 2 tablespoons unsalted butter
- 40 g (¼ cup) pine nuts
- 150 g full-fat Greek yoghurt, chilled

TO SERVE

- dill fronds
- coriander leaves
- mint leaves

Preheat the oven to 200°C fan-forced.

Place the chicken, za'atar, cumin, allspice, sumac, lemon zest and juice, garlic and olive oil in a large non-reactive bowl. Season and rub everything into the chicken very well. Set aside.

Place the potato on a large baking tray. Squeeze the tomatoes over the potato and toss to coat. Drizzle with a little olive oil and season. Place the chicken, skin-side up, on and around the potato, drizzling over any of the marinade remaining in the bowl. Roast for 1 hour or until the chicken and potato are cooked.

Melt the butter in a small saucepan, add the pine nuts and fry until they are golden.

Spoon the chilled yoghurt onto the chicken and top with the hot buttery pine nuts. Finish by scattering on the dill, coriander and mint and a sprinkle of extra sumac.

SERVES 4–6

VINEGAR MAPLE CHICKEN

WITH FENNEL

- 4 chicken marylands (around 1.4 kg)
- 2 red onions, quartered
- 1 fennel bulb, cut into wedges, fronds reserved
- 80 ml (⅓ cup) malt vinegar
- 2½ tablespoons maple syrup
- 1 tablespoon extra-virgin olive oil, plus extra for drizzling
- 1 teaspoon fennel seeds, crushed
- 1 teaspoon coriander seeds, crushed
- 4 cardamom pods, bruised
- 2 garlic cloves, finely grated
- finely grated zest and juice of 1 lime, plus extra lime wedges to serve
- sea salt and white pepper
- coriander leaves, to serve

A simple one-tray chicken dish with some big flavours: sweetness from the maple syrup, sourness from the malt vinegar and warmth from the fennel, coriander and cardamom. This is wonderful served simply with some steamed rice or flatbread.

Preheat the oven to 190°C fan-forced.

Place the chicken, onion, fennel wedges, vinegar, maple syrup, olive oil, spices, garlic, lime zest and juice and a good pinch of salt and white pepper in a large bowl and use your hands to massage the mixture into the chicken and vegetables. Season with more salt and pepper.

Place the onion and fennel in a shallow roasting tin and nestle in the chicken, skin-side up. Pour any remaining marinade onto the chicken. Roast for 1 hour or until the chicken is golden and cooked through. Top with the reserved fennel fronds and the coriander leaves and serve with the lime wedges.

SERVES 4–6

CHICKEN SALTIMBOCCA

Literally meaning 'jump in the mouth', saltimbocca is one of the most inimitable dishes hailing from Rome. I've opted for chicken breasts here, but veal, if you prefer, is the traditional choice. I love to make these for a weeknight dinner where I want something simple and quick, but also just that little bit special if friends or family are over.

- 3 skinless chicken breasts (approximately 750 g)
- sea salt and black pepper
- 200 g finely sliced prosciutto crudo
- around 14 sage leaves, plus extra for frying
- plain flour, for dusting
- 1 tablespoon extra-virgin olive oil
- 80 g cold unsalted butter, cubed
- 3 tablespoons dry white wine

Slice the chicken breasts horizontally into 1 cm thick pieces. You should get three or four pieces per breast. Now use a meat mallet or the base of a heavy mug to gently flatten each piece of chicken to around 5 mm thick. Season with salt and pepper.

If you have toothpicks, first place a slice of prosciutto on a piece of chicken and then add a sage leaf, securing it with a toothpick. Alternatively, place a sage leaf directly on a piece of chicken and top it with a slice of prosciutto, pressing the prosciutto onto the chicken to secure the sage. Repeat with the remaining chicken, prosciutto and sage.

Dust the underside of the chicken pieces with the flour, shaking off any excess.

Heat the olive oil and 1 tablespoon of the butter in a large frying pan over a medium–high heat. Working in batches, add the chicken, sage-side down, and cook for 1–2 minutes or until the prosciutto is starting to colour, then turn over and cook for 1 minute more. Pour the wine around the chicken and continue cooking for 1–2 minutes or until the chicken is lightly golden underneath and cooked through. Transfer the chicken to a serving plate.

Add the remaining cold butter and the extra sage leaves to the pan, swirl the butter around to create a sauce and cook for 2 minutes or until the sauce has thickened slightly. Pour the sauce over the chicken saltimbocca and serve.

SERVES 4

PORK COTOLETTA

WITH SAUCE VIERGE

I can still remember one of my best primary school friend's mum's cotolette. She would make what seemed to be hundreds of them using disposable foil trays: one for the egg and milk, one for the flour and one for the crumbs. Then, beside the crumbing trays would be another very large one, lined with stale white supermarket bread to drain the cotolette. I never found out if she bought the bread specifically for this purpose or if it was left over and had become stale, but either way, that image is seared into my memory. I make my cotolette on a much smaller scale, and like to serve them with a refreshing sauce vierge to cut through the richness. Sauce vierge, essentially a tomato vinaigrette, is a great recipe to have up your sleeve as it also goes well with grilled meats or fish. This dish is one of my favourites to make for Saturday lunch after coming home from the market.

- 4 × 200 g boneless pork cutlets, rind removed
- sea salt and black pepper
- 2 eggs, lightly beaten
- 1 tablespoon full-cream milk
- plain flour, for dusting
- 100 g Japanese breadcrumbs (panko), for crumbing
- neutral vegetable oil, for frying
- broadleaf rocket leaves, to serve

SAUCE VIERGE

- 300 g cherry tomatoes, diced
- 1 tablespoon salted capers, rinsed and drained
- 2 shallots, finely diced
- small handful of basil leaves, roughly chopped
- 2 tablespoons extra-virgin olive oil
- 1 tablespoon red wine vinegar
- sea salt

Combine the sauce vierge ingredients in a small bowl and set aside.

Flatten the pork cutlets using a meat mallet or the base of a heavy mug. Season with salt and pepper.

Whisk the eggs and milk in a shallow bowl. Sprinkle a layer of flour into another shallow bowl and place the breadcrumbs in a third shallow bowl. Working with one cutlet at a time, and keeping one hand clean, dust a cutlet in the flour, shaking off any excess, then dip in the egg mix and finish with a coating of the breadcrumbs, patting them on to ensure they stick. Transfer to a plate and repeat with the remaining cutlets.

Heat 2 cm of vegetable oil in a large deep frying pan over a medium–high heat. Add the crumbed pork, in batches, and fry for 2–3 minutes on each side or until golden and cooked through. Drain on a wire rack and season with some salt.

Serve the cotolette with the sauce vierge and rocket leaves on the side.

SERVES 4

STUFFED CABBAGE
WITH SAUSAGE & PORCINI

Here, two humble ingredients – sausages and cabbage – are turned into the most glorious and intensely flavoured parcel. This recipe was the very first idea I had for this book. It was inspired by memories of a Christmas spent in Jura, France, with the rough recipe sitting in one of my notebooks for years. Impressively beautiful, chou farci, or stuffed cabbage, is such a humble show stopper. While chou farci may have originally been created to use up leftover roast meats, mine utilises sausage meat instead.

The earthiness of the porcini really ties everything together and the sausages are just so full of flavour. The preparation may seem a little intimidating, but once the cabbage leaves are blanched and the vegetables sautéed, it really is rather quick. It is one of my favourite things to prepare in winter, when savoy cabbages are easily found and I want something ever so comforting. I make mine in a round copper pan, but even a round cake tin works well. Smaller individual parcels can be made, too, although they will need to be wrapped in twine and baked in a dish where they can fit snugly together. Chou farci is wonderful served with mashed potatoes or simply with some crusty bread on the side.

- 1 savoy cabbage (approximately 800 g–1 kg)
- 10 g dried porcini mushrooms
- 2 tablespoons unsalted butter, plus extra for greasing and dotting
- 1 tablespoon extra-virgin olive oil
- 2 leeks, white and pale green parts, roughly diced
- ½ teaspoon fennel seeds, toasted and crushed
- sea salt
- large handful of parsley leaves, finely chopped
- black pepper
- 6 continental pork sausages, casings removed

Preheat the oven to 180°C fan-forced. Grease a 20 cm round, deep-sided ovenproof dish with butter.

Keeping them intact, remove eight of the nicest, darkest outer leaves of the cabbage. Weigh the remaining cabbage (you will need 500 g) and roughly chop. Set aside.

Blanch the cabbage leaves in a large saucepan of salted boiling water for 3–4 minutes or until bright green and pliable. Remove carefully and drain on clean tea towels.

Place the porcini in a small bowl and ladle in just enough of the hot cabbage cooking water to cover them. Soak for 10 minutes, then remove from the liquid, roughly chop and set aside. Reserve the soaking liquid.

Warm the butter and olive oil in a large frying pan over a medium heat. Add the leek, fennel seeds and a pinch of salt and cook for 6–7 minutes or until the leek begins to soften and colour. Add the chopped cabbage, stir to coat and cook for 2–3 minutes. When the cabbage begins to collapse, add the porcini and the reserved soaking liquid and cook until all the liquid has evaporated and the cabbage is quite tender, around 8–10 minutes. Stir in the parsley, season to taste and allow to cool.

Choose your nicest blanched cabbage leaf and place it in the base of the dish. Place three or four more cabbage leaves on top of the first leaf, rotating their direction to ensure they line the base and come up the side of the dish.

Spoon half the leek and cabbage mixture into the dish and even out with the back of a spoon. Take half the sausage meat, flatten it out to form a large patty-like shape and place it on the leek and cabbage layer. Repeat this layering process with the remaining leek and cabbage mixture and sausage meat.

Cover the meat layer with the remaining cabbage leaves and bring the overhanging leaves in towards the centre to enclose the parcel. Dot a little extra butter over the cabbage and roast for 45–50 minutes or until the cabbage is deep golden in colour and the centre is hot. To test, poke the centre of the parcel with a knife; if the knife feels hot, it's ready.

Allow the stuffed cabbage to rest for 10 minutes, then invert it onto a large serving plate, being careful as it will be hot and juicy.

SERVES 4–6

Recipe images overleaf

ROAST PORK

WITH CANNELLINI BEANS & SAGE

There is something rather satisfying about the combination of pork and beans. Here, the beans are cooked in chicken stock with garlic and sage for an intense flavour base to the rich and crispy-skinned pork. The cherry tomatoes are roasted for a real concentration of flavour and are then met with some English spinach leaves. The beans actually go very well with roast chicken or grilled fish, too.

- 1 × 6-point pork loin rack (around 1 kg), rind scored
- 200 g dried cannellini beans, soaked overnight in water, then drained
- 1.5 litres chicken stock
- 3 garlic cloves, whole and unpeeled
- 10 sage leaves
- 100 ml dry white wine
- sea salt
- 400 g cherry tomatoes, halved
- 2 tablespoons extra-virgin olive oil, plus extra for drizzling
- 1 bunch of English spinach, thick stems trimmed and leaves roughly chopped
- finely grated zest of 1 lemon

Pat the pork dry with paper towel, place in a roasting tin and sit, uncovered, overnight in the fridge to dry out.

Place the cannellini beans, stock, garlic and half the sage in a large saucepan over a medium–high heat. Bring to the boil, then reduce the heat to low and simmer for around 1 hour, or until the beans are very tender and the stock is reduced.

Bring the pork to room temperature. Preheat the oven to 180°C fan-forced. Line a baking tray with baking paper.

Add the wine, the remaining sage and 150 ml of water to the tray, being careful not to pour directly onto the pork. Rub some salt onto the pork rind and a little onto the flesh. Roast for 65–70 minutes or until the internal temperature of the pork reaches 63°C on an instant-read thermometer. Allow to rest.

Meanwhile, arrange the cherry tomatoes, cut-side up, on the tray. Drizzle on the olive oil, season with salt and roast for 30 minutes.

While the pork is resting, gently warm the beans and add the spinach. Cook for 3–4 minutes or until the spinach is wilted. Add the lemon zest and season to taste with salt.

Spoon the cannellini beans onto a serving plate, cut the pork into individual cutlets and serve on top of the beans with the roasted cherry tomatoes and a drizzle of olive oil.

SERVES 6

LAMB MEATBALLS

WITH BAGNETTO VERDE

- 60 g stale bread, crusts removed
- 80 ml (⅓ cup) full-cream milk
- 750 g lamb mince
- 2 garlic cloves, finely grated
- ½ teaspoon freshly grated nutmeg
- 40 g Parmigiano Reggiano, finely grated, plus extra to serve
- 30 g Pecorino Romano, finely grated
- large handful of parsley leaves, finely chopped
- 1 egg, lightly whisked
- sea salt and black pepper

BAGNETTO VERDE

- 1 garlic clove, peeled
- sea salt
- 60 g parsley leaves (from about 1½ bunches)
- 60 g mint leaves (from about 1½ bunches)
- 4 anchovy fillets in olive oil, drained
- 1 hard-boiled egg yolk
- 50 g fresh breadcrumbs
- 80 ml (⅓ cup) white wine vinegar
- 200 ml extra-virgin olive oil, plus extra for frying
- black pepper

Bagnetto verde is a green sauce from Piemonte in northern Italy. It's punchy, vibrant and a wonderful accompaniment to these lamb meatballs, which are simply flavoured with parsley, cheese and nutmeg. They are very much inspired by the polpette di Teresa from one of my favourite lunch spots in Rome – Trattoria da Cesare. On a recent trip, I ate them with a simple salad of puntarelle dressed with garlic and anchovies. A heavenly memory.

Place the bread in a small bowl and cover with the milk. Allow to soak for 10–15 minutes. Squeeze the excess milk from the bread, then crumble it into a large bowl. Add the mince, garlic, nutmeg, cheeses, parsley and egg. Season with salt and pepper and mix with your hands until well combined. Roll into golf ball–sized balls and place on a tray. Refrigerate for 30 minutes.

Meanwhile, for the bagnetto verde, pound the garlic with a pinch of salt using a mortar and pestle. Add the herbs and continue pounding. Finally, add the anchovies and egg yolk and pound until you have a fairly homogeneous paste. Stir in the breadcrumbs, vinegar and olive oil. Season to taste and set aside. Alternatively, blitz the garlic, herbs, anchovies and egg yolk in a food processor until finely chopped. Add the breadcrumbs, season with salt and pepper and, with the motor running, add the vinegar and olive oil.

Warm a few tablespoons of extra olive oil in a large frying pan over a medium heat. Add the meatballs and pan-fry, turning them often to ensure they brown on all sides, for 4–5 minutes or until cooked. Serve the meatballs with a grating of extra Parmigiano Reggiano and the bagnetto verde.

SERVES 4

MARINATED SPICED LAMB

WITH CUCUMBER YOGHURT

- 12 lamb loin chops
- 2 teaspoons sumac
- 2 garlic cloves, finely grated
- finely grated zest and juice of 1 lemon
- 2 tablespoons extra-virgin olive oil, plus extra for drizzling
- sea salt and black pepper

BAHĀRĀT

- 2 tablespoons cumin seeds
- 2 tablespoons coriander seeds
- 1 cinnamon stick, broken
- 2 teaspoons black peppercorns
- 1 teaspoon cloves
- 6 cardamom pods
- 2 allspice berries
- 1 teaspoon freshly grated nutmeg

CUCUMBER YOGHURT

- 3 Lebanese cucumbers
- sea salt
- 350 g full-fat Greek yoghurt
- 1 garlic clove, finely grated
- 1 teaspoon sumac, plus extra for sprinkling
- handful of dill fronds, finely chopped, plus extra to serve
- handful of mint leaves, finely chopped, plus extra to serve
- 1 teaspoon dried mint
- juice of ½ lemon
- black pepper

Somewhere between Greek tzatziki and Lebanese khyar bi laban, this cucumber yoghurt sauce is the perfect accompaniment to spiced lamb. Here, I have chosen loin chops, but cutlets or chump chops are perfect, too. Bahārāt simply means 'spices' in Arabic, and is a spice blend that varies depending on the region or family. I make my own at home, but it is readily available from Middle Eastern and select grocers.

For the bahārāt, place all the whole spices in a mortar and bash with the pestle until the cardamom pods open. Discard the papery outer pod and continue to grind until you have a fairly fine mix. Alternatively, use a spice grinder. Stir in the nutmeg. Store the bahārāt in an airtight jar for up to 1 year.

Place the lamb in a large non-reactive bowl and add 1 tablespoon of bahārāt, the sumac, garlic, lemon zest and juice and olive oil. Use your hands to rub the marinade into the lamb, ensuring it is well coated. Season well, then transfer to the fridge to marinate for at least 1 hour or up to 4 hours. Bring to room temperature before cooking.

Meanwhile, for the cucumber yoghurt, coarsely grate the cucumbers and sit them in a colander over a bowl. Sprinkle over a good pinch of salt and toss to disperse it. Allow to sit and drain for 10–15 minutes. Squeeze out any excess liquid and transfer the cucumber to a bowl, along with the yoghurt, garlic, sumac, herbs and lemon juice. Season to taste, drizzle with some olive oil and top with a sprinkling of extra sumac.

Preheat a barbecue grill or chargrill pan over a medium–high heat. Cook the lamb chops for 5–6 minutes, turning halfway, until cooked to your liking. Allow to rest for 6–8 minutes, then serve with the cucumber yoghurt and extra dill and mint.

SERVES 4–6

CHARGRILLED MARINATED LAMB LEG

WITH ROMESCO

This recipe is one I lean on a lot – the marinade, which uses a whole lemon, pith and all, gives such a sensational amount of complexity to the lamb. It is not at all bitter, and, once grilled, has a gentle hum of sweetness. It's surprising in all the right ways and I have had much success using it for marinating chicken, too. Romesco is one of my best-loved things – traditionally served with fish, which is superb, but also as I do here with lamb. It's smoky, a little spicy and just so irresistible that I often make a double batch to keep some for the week.

- 1 × 1.3 kg butterflied leg of lamb, fat scored
- 1 lemon, halved and seeds removed
- large handful of parsley leaves and stems, plus extra roughly chopped parsley leaves to serve
- 3 garlic cloves, crushed with the side of a knife
- 2 tablespoons extra-virgin olive oil, plus extra for drizzling
- sea salt and black pepper

ROMESCO

- 3 roma tomatoes
- 2 red capsicums
- 2 garlic cloves
- sea salt
- 80 g (½ cup) toasted blanched almonds
- 30 g fresh breadcrumbs
- pinch of chilli flakes or Aleppo pepper
- 1 teaspoon sweet smoked paprika
- 2 tablespoons extra-virgin olive oil
- sherry vinegar, to taste

Place the lamb in a large bowl and set aside. Place the lemon, parsley leaves and stems, garlic and olive oil in a food processor, season with salt and pepper and blitz to a fine puree. Pour over the lamb and rub in with your hands to ensure the lamb is well coated. Cover and refrigerate for 2–3 hours.

Preheat the oven to 180°C fan-forced.

For the romesco, place the tomatoes and whole capsicums on a baking tray and roast in the oven for 1 hour or until they have collapsed and the skins are blistered and charred. When cool enough to handle, remove the skin, seeds and membrane from the capsicums. Peel the tomatoes and set the flesh aside. Pound the garlic with a pinch of salt using a mortar and pestle to create a paste. Add the almonds and continue to pound. Now add the roasted tomatoes and capsicums and pound again. Stir in the breadcrumbs, chilli flakes or Aleppo pepper and smoked paprika, along with the olive oil and enough vinegar to create some tartness. I like to add around 1 tablespoon, but it will depend on how sweet the tomato and capsicum are. Season to taste with salt and set aside.

Bring the lamb to room temperature. Preheat a barbecue grill to medium–high or heat a chargrill pan over a medium–high heat. Add the lamb and cook for 20–25 minutes, turning halfway, until the lamb is cooked to medium. Allow to rest, then slice and arrange on a serving plate. Serve with the romesco, the extra chopped parsley and a drizzle of extra olive oil.

SERVES 4–6

BEEF TAGLIATA

WITH TONNATO SAUCE

A play on the classic vitello tonnato, this beef tagliata with tonnato sauce keeps many of the same ideas from the original. However, instead of poaching a piece of veal, I've chosen beef in the form of sirloin steaks, which are more readily available. The tonnato sauce – salty, briny and fresh – is a quick concoction that really works here, drizzled over the steak nestled among peppery rocket leaves and shavings of Parmigiano Reggiano.

- 3 × 250 g sirloin steaks
- sea salt
- broadleaf rocket leaves, to serve
- shaved Parmigiano Reggiano, to serve

TONNATO SAUCE

- 125 g canned tuna in olive oil, drained
- juice of 1 lemon
- 2 teaspoons salted capers, rinsed and drained, plus extra to serve
- 2 anchovy fillets
- 150 ml extra-virgin olive oil, plus extra for drizzling
- sea salt and black pepper

For the tonnato sauce, place the tuna, lemon juice, capers and anchovies in a blender or food processor and blitz until combined. With the motor running, slowly stream in the olive oil. If the mixture is too thick, add a little water and blitz again. Season to taste and set aside.

Preheat a barbecue grill or chargrill pan over a medium–high heat. Season the steaks with salt and drizzle a little extra olive oil over both sides. Grill the steaks for 5 minutes on each side or until medium rare. Remove from the pan and rest for 5–8 minutes. Cut the steaks into 1 cm thick slices and arrange on a serving plate with the rocket. Top with the shaved Parmigiano Reggiano, the tonnato sauce and some extra capers.

SERVES 4–6

BRAISED BEEF RIBS

WITH GREMOLATA & SOFT POLENTA

In the depths of winter, I often crave polenta. Thick, rich and supremely satisfying, it also happens to be very economical. Topped with braised beef ribs brightened with a punchy gremolata, this really is a dish to bring comfort. The ribs need quite a while in the oven, but the result is truly worth it.

- 2 kg beef short ribs, cut into 6 cm pieces
- sea salt
- 1 tablespoon extra-virgin olive oil
- 1 onion, diced
- 1 carrot, diced
- 2 celery stalks, diced
- 3 garlic cloves, whole and unpeeled
- 3 thyme sprigs
- 2 fresh bay leaves
- 2 parsley stalks
- 2 oregano sprigs
- 400 ml red wine
- 200 g canned tomato polpa (finely crushed tomatoes)
- 650 ml light chicken stock or water
- 1 tablespoon red wine vinegar
- 1 star anise

GREMOLATA

- handful of parsley leaves
- 2 garlic cloves, crushed with the side of a knife
- finely grated zest of 1 lemon

SOFT POLENTA

- sea salt
- 200 g polenta
- 30 g Parmigiano Reggiano, grated
- 3 tablespoons pure cream

Preheat the oven to 175°C fan-forced.

Season the ribs with salt and set aside.

Heat the olive oil in a large cast-iron Dutch oven over a medium–high heat. Add the beef, in batches if needed, and brown on all sides, then remove from the dish. Drain all but 1 tablespoon of fat from the dish. Reduce the heat to medium–low and add the onion, carrot, celery and garlic. Gently cook for 7–8 minutes or until the vegetables are softened. Add the herbs and cook for 2–3 minutes longer or until fragrant.

Increase the heat to medium–high, deglaze with the wine, scraping the bottom of the dish to lift any brown bits, and simmer for 1–2 minutes. Add the tomatoes, 500 ml (2 cups) of stock or water, the vinegar and star anise and bring to a simmer, then return the beef to the dish. Cover and transfer to the oven to cook for 2½–3 hours, or until the liquid has reduced and the beef is very tender.

For the gremolata, finely chop the parsley, then layer on the garlic and continue chopping until you have a fine mixture. Add the lemon zest and mix through, then transfer to a bowl.

About 1 hour before the beef is cooked, begin the soft polenta. Bring 1 litre of water to the boil in a large saucepan over a high heat. Season with salt and rain in the polenta, stirring with a wooden spoon or whisk. Continue to stir until creamy and the mixture comes to the boil. Reduce to the lowest heat possible, cover and cook for 40–45 minutes or until the polenta is cooked. Check every now and again to ensure there is enough water, adding a little boiling water if needed. Once ready, stir through the Parmigiano Reggiano and cream and keep warm.

Remove the beef from the dish and keep warm. Strain the liquid into a bowl or jug, reserving the vegetables and discarding the woody herbs and star anise. Skim (and discard) the excess oil from the surface with a large spoon – there will be quite a lot. Return the oil-free braising liquid to the dish along with the remaining 150 ml of stock or water. Simmer, whisking to combine, for 2–3 minutes or until slightly reduced. Return the vegetables to the pan to warm through. Check for seasoning.

Transfer the polenta to a serving plate and spoon on the beef and the pan juices. Top with the gremolata and serve.

SERVES 4–6

CHAPTER FIVE

Salads & vegetables

Each season is as exciting as the last and makes way for new recipes, opportunities and moments.

ACQUASALE

- 3 Lebanese cucumbers, peeled and thickly sliced on the diagonal
- ½ red onion, roughly chopped
- 3 very nice ripe tomatoes, roughly chopped
- 3 slices of stale sourdough bread, roughly torn, or 2 friselle, roughly broken
- small handful of oregano leaves
- 80 ml (⅓ cup) extra-virgin olive oil
- 2 tablespoons red wine vinegar
- sea salt and black pepper

It might seem counterintuitive to add water to a salad, but the result is refreshing and utterly delicious. I first ate this salad in the Pugliese countryside where I stayed for a few weeks. It was made with friselle, a twice-baked bread synonymous with the region. If you can find friselle, they are fantastic and hold the liquid so well due to how dry they initially are. This tomato and bread salad is wonderful to eat on very hot days, even if you're not by the pool in Puglia.

Place the cucumber, onion, tomato, sourdough or friselle and oregano in a large bowl and toss to combine.

Whisk 100 ml of water with the olive oil and vinegar in a small bowl. Season to taste and pour over the salad. Use your hands to toss everything with the dressing. Allow to sit for 10 minutes, then serve.

SERVES 4

ITALIAN FLAT BEANS

WITH MINT & RICOTTA SALATA

A simple salad with a punchy vinaigrette that cuts through richness, this is perfect for serving alongside grilled meats or roast chicken. If you can't find Italian flat beans, sometimes called Roman beans or runner beans, French green beans are more than fine. I love the fluffiness of the ricotta salata, but a cloud of grated Parmigiano Reggiano or Pecorino Romano works equally well.

- 500 g Italian flat beans, trimmed and cut into 8–10 cm lengths
- 3 tablespoons extra-virgin olive oil
- 1 tablespoon red wine vinegar
- 2 shallots, finely diced
- sea salt and black pepper
- large handful of mint leaves, roughly chopped
- finely grated ricotta salata, to serve

Blanch the beans in a large saucepan of salted boiling water for 3–4 minutes or until bright green and tender. Refresh in iced water, then pat dry and place in a bowl.

Whisk the olive oil and vinegar in a small bowl and add the shallot. Season to taste with salt and pepper.

Dress the beans with the vinaigrette and arrange on a serving plate. Scatter on the mint leaves and plenty of ricotta salata and serve.

SERVES 4

ROASTED FENNEL

WITH CHERRY TOMATOES & OREGANO

The first time I ever ate fennel was in the middle of a bustling market in Catania, Sicily. I was eighteen and Malta-bound for Christmas. It was the beginning of a three-month backpacking adventure in Europe. I stood in the market with my sister, just there for the day, so with no real ability to buy anything substantial to cook with. Some citrus to eat on the boat was a high priority. But drawn to one of the stallholders' large mound of fennel, pure white and wispy green, my sister, who had been living in Italy and spoke perfect Italian, struck up a conversation. He cut off some raw fennel for us to eat and there we were, in the centre of this hive of activity, munching on a wedge of raw fennel. I love the gentle anise flavour of fennel when it is raw and how sweet it becomes when it is braised or roasted, even better with cherry tomatoes and oregano. This is a simple vegetable dish, but that is the beauty of it. Perfectly uncomplicated.

- 2 fennel bulbs, cut into wedges, some fronds reserved
- 200 g cherry tomatoes
- 3 oregano sprigs
- 3 garlic cloves
- 2 tablespoons extra-virgin olive oil, plus extra for drizzling
- 2½ tablespoons dry white wine
- sea salt

Preheat the oven to 180°C fan-forced.

Place the fennel, cherry tomatoes, oregano and garlic in a roasting tin. You want the fennel wedges to sit rather snugly in the tin as they will shrink as they cook. Drizzle on the olive oil and wine and season to taste.

Wet a piece of baking paper and scrunch it to soften. Unfurl the paper and place over the vegetables to cover. Roast for 40 minutes. Remove the paper, increase the oven temperature to 200°C fan-forced and continue to roast, turning occasionally to encourage even cooking, for 20–25 minutes or until the fennel is tender and the tomatoes have completely collapsed and are beginning to caramelise. Top with a drizzle of extra olive oil and the reserved fennel fronds.

SERVES 4

STILTON, WALNUT & GRAPE SALAD

- 150 g red or black grapes, halved
- 3 celery stalks, finely sliced on the diagonal
- 100 g Stilton or other blue cheese, crumbled
- 60 g (½ cup) walnuts, toasted and roughly chopped
- small handful of parsley leaves, roughly chopped
- handful of broadleaf rocket leaves

DRESSING

- juice of 2 oranges
- 2 tablespoons extra-virgin olive oil
- 1 tablespoon red wine vinegar
- sea salt and black pepper, to taste

I like to make this salad at the beginning of autumn when local grapes appear at the shops. It's so simple in nature, yet the combination of the salty, funky Stilton with the crunch of walnuts and celery and the sweet musky flavour of the grapes is a triumph. Reducing the citrus juice elevates the dressing and is a wonderful tip I learned from the talented cook Julie Marr, who I spent some time cooking with in Puglia. It is well worth finding broadleaf rocket for this salad as it is light and peppery, but regular rocket will work fine, too.

Place the grapes, celery, cheese, walnuts, parsley and rocket in a bowl and set aside.

For the dressing, place the orange juice in a small saucepan over a medium heat and bring to a simmer. Cook for 4–5 minutes or until reduced by half. Place in a jar, along with the olive oil, vinegar and salt and pepper, and shake vigorously.

Pour the dressing over the salad and toss to combine. Transfer to a serving plate and serve.

SERVES 4

FRESH BORLOTTI BEANS

I am usually all for canned beans and legumes, but borlotti beans from a can are often disappointingly mushy. When fresh borlotti beans are in season, absolutely nothing can compare to their beauty, texture and flavour. The joy of podding them and unveiling their motley crimson speckles never gets old. While they do lose their magic pattern once cooked, the sight of a freshly cooked bowl of borlotti beans, bathing in good olive oil, almost gives me butterflies. It's nostalgic, comforting and the most perfect accompaniment to grilled or roasted fish or meat, or added into salads with some canned fish.

- 1 kg fresh borlotti beans, podded, or 500 g podded borlotti beans
- 3–4 fresh bay leaves
- 1 tablespoon extra-virgin olive oil, plus extra for drizzling
- 2 rosemary, sage or oregano sprigs
- 3 whole garlic cloves
- sea salt

Place all the ingredients, except for the salt, in a large saucepan and cover with 2 litres of cold water. Bring to the boil over high heat, then reduce the heat to low and simmer for 30–35 minutes or until the borlotti beans are tender. Skim the water of any impurities that rise to the surface during the first 10 minutes or as needed.

Now, depending on your preference, you can enjoy the beans in two ways.

If you want them brothy, simply season the beans with salt and serve drizzled with some extra olive oil.

Alternatively, strain the beans and reserve the liquid for another use (it is great added to soups instead of stock). Transfer the warm beans and aromatics to a serving bowl, season with salt and drizzle on plenty of extra olive oil.

SERVES 4–6

PEAR & WITLOF SALAD

Witlof, also known as endive, Belgian endive or chicory, is such an underrated vegetable. Closely related to Italian radicchio, witlof is slightly bitter but also mildly sweet and wonderful cooked or raw. I love adding the leaves to a plate of raw vegetables to dip into good olive oil or layering them on a plate for a salad. Because of their subtle bitterness, fruit is a welcome addition and works so well. Pears are fantastic here, but apples are lovely, too. The dressing is zingy, creamy and fills every witlof leaf as if it were a cup. Slice the pear just before serving to avoid it oxidising. I like to layer the salad on a fairly flat platter, so every mouthful contains some of the witlof, pear, chives and almonds.

- 1 witlof, leaves separated
- 1 pear, quartered, cored and finely sliced
- small handful of chives, finely chopped
- 40 g toasted flaked almonds
- sea salt and black pepper

CRÈME FRAÎCHE DRESSING

- 1 tablespoon crème fraîche
- 3 tablespoons extra-virgin olive oil
- 1 teaspoon red wine vinegar
- sea salt and black pepper

Combine all the crème fraîche dressing ingredients in a bowl and whisk to emulsify. Taste and adjust seasoning.

Arrange the witlof and pear on a serving plate in a single layer. Pour on the dressing, then top with the chives and toasted flaked almonds. Season with salt and pepper and serve.

SERVES 4

ROMAN STUFFED TOMATOES

When I lived in Tuscany, I used to take a train into Rome on my day off; the Tuscan countryside was only an hour or so away. From Roma Termini, I would stop for breakfast (a cappuccino and a cornetto) and walk through Monti to Piazza Navona and the Jewish Quarter. Along the way, I would stop at all my favourite shops. By the end of the day I would have procured cheese, pizza bianca, a bottle of local-ish wine and a tray of these stuffed tomatoes. I would buy them from a tavola calda (a deli-like establishment with pre-prepared foods to be taken home and reheated). Each week I would visit the same one, sometimes for the artichokes braised with wine and mint or the grilled and marinated zucchini, but usually it was for the stuffed tomatoes and potatoes. Everything cooks together, the rice, potatoes and tomatoes seem to harmoniously all be ready at the same time. Make these when tomatoes are very much in season and gorgeously red.

- 6 tomatoes (around 1 kg)
- 100 g Carnaroli rice or other risotto rice
- small handful of basil leaves, finely chopped
- small handful of oregano or marjoram leaves, finely chopped
- 2 garlic cloves, finely grated
- 80 ml (⅓ cup) extra-virgin olive oil
- sea salt and black pepper
- 800 g desiree potatoes, peeled

Preheat the oven to 190°C fan-forced.

Working with one tomato at a time, cut the tomato about 1 cm from the stem to create a base and a lid. Scoop the flesh out from the tomato base, finely chop and place it in a bowl. Set aside the now-hollow base and the lid. Repeat with the remaining tomatoes.

Add the rice, basil, oregano or marjoram, garlic and 2 tablespoons of the olive oil to the bowl of tomato flesh. Season to taste and set aside.

Cut the potatoes into fat chips or wedges and arrange on a baking tray. Drizzle on 1 tablespoon of the remaining olive oil, season with salt and toss to coat. Add the tomato bases to the tray, nestling them around the potatoes. Spoon the rice mixture into the tomato bases, then top each with a tomato lid. Drizzle on the remaining 1 tablespoon of olive oil. Bake for 1 hour or until the potatoes are cooked and the rice is tender, then serve.

SERVES 6

CUCUMBER, FETA & CABBAGE SALAD

I love the combination of crunchy cabbage, fresh cucumber and salty feta. It's undoubtedly a simple salad, and one of my very favourites. The dill, in my opinion, is really what makes this dish so wonderful, so don't be alarmed by the amount – it's one of the stars. Once dressed, the cabbage and cucumber begin to soften a little, but in a good way, making this a perfect salad to take on a picnic or eat across a couple of days.

- ¼ white cabbage (400 g), finely shredded
- 4 Lebanese cucumbers, sliced into 3 mm rounds
- 1 bunch of dill, fronds finely chopped
- 200 g Greek feta, crumbled
- 3–4 shallots, finely sliced
- 80 ml (⅓ cup) extra-virgin olive oil
- juice of 1 lemon
- sea salt and black pepper

Place the cabbage, cucumber, dill, feta and shallot in a large bowl and toss to combine. Pour on the olive oil and lemon juice and season to taste.

Mix the salad very well and serve.

SERVES 4

POTATO & SILVERBEET AL FORNO

In the depths of winter, there is nothing more comforting than a dish of bubbling baked potatoes brought to the table. Creamy, rich and an absolute go-to, my version adds some cooked silverbeet to the base of the dish. I like to add in some greens as they not only provide another opportunity to use the silverbeet I grow, but I also like the contrast in textures they bring to the dish. I use quite a large dish for this recipe, but it works equally well in a slightly smaller one, which will give you more layers.

- unsalted butter, for greasing
- 1 bunch of silverbeet, ribs removed and reserved for another use
- 350 ml pure cream
- ½ teaspoon freshly grated nutmeg
- 2 thyme sprigs, leaves picked
- 3 sage leaves, roughly torn
- sea salt and black pepper
- 1.2 kg potatoes (such as Dutch cream, nicola or desiree), peeled
- 60 g Parmigiano Reggiano, finely grated

Preheat the oven to 180°C fan-forced. Grease a 40 cm oval baking dish with butter and set aside.

Blanch the silverbeet leaves in boiling water for 3–4 minutes. Drain and cool under cold water or in an ice bath. Squeeze the excess moisture from the silverbeet and roughly chop. Scatter the silverbeet over the base of the dish.

Combine the cream, nutmeg, thyme and sage in a large bowl and season well.

Finely slice the potatoes on a mandoline, about 2–3 mm thick. Place the potato in the bowl with the cream mixture and use your hands to ensure all the slices are coated. Place a layer of potato, slightly overlapping the slices, on the silverbeet. Scatter on one-quarter of the Parmigiano Reggiano, then add another layer of potato and another one-quarter of Parmigiano Reggiano. Add one more layer of potato and pour any remaining cream mixture over the top. Finish with the remaining Parmigiano Reggiano and bake for 60–65 minutes or until the potato is tender when poked with a knife. Allow to sit for 10 minutes, then serve.

SERVES 6–8

ZUCCHINI, BROAD BEAN & FREEKEH SALAD

Freekeh is green wheat, roasted and rubbed to give a sturdy fragrant grain. It is a wonderful addition to a salad of grilled zucchini and broad beans. Heavy with herbs, this gorgeous dish is perfect when the zucchini are young and tender. If you grow or can find some zucchini flowers, don't hesitate to include them – they add beautiful colour and a lovely sweetness. A celebration of the end of spring and beginning of summer, this salad brings together so many things I love. It's substantial, vibrant and also has a richness to it, which means it can be a meal all by itself.

- 2 tablespoons extra-virgin olive oil, plus extra as needed
- 4 young zucchini (around 600 g), halved lengthways and cut into 3 cm pieces
- sea salt
- 650 g broad beans, podded, or 350 g podded broad beans
- 80 g freekeh, rinsed
- 2 shallots, finely sliced
- large handful of dill fronds, roughly chopped
- large handful of mint leaves, roughly chopped
- juice of 1 lemon
- ½ teaspoon sumac
- 1 tablespoon unsalted butter
- 50 g slivered almonds

Heat the olive oil in a large frying pan over a medium heat. Add the zucchini and a pinch of salt and cook, turning often, for 10–12 minutes or until the zucchini is golden on all sides and tender. Transfer to a large bowl and allow to cool.

Blanch the broad beans in a saucepan of salted boiling water for 2–3 minutes, then refresh in iced water. Smaller broad beans can be left in their skin, but double pod any larger beans and add to the bowl with the zucchini. Set aside.

Cook the freekeh in a small saucepan of salted boiling water until tender, around 20 minutes. Drain very well, then add to the zucchini and broad beans, along with the shallot, dill and mint. Toss to combine. Add the lemon juice and sumac and season to taste with salt. You can add some more olive oil here if you like, but I tend not to since there is melted butter to come.

Melt the butter in a small frying pan over a medium heat, add the almonds and cook, stirring often, until golden.

Arrange the salad on a serving plate and top with the buttery almonds.

SERVES 4

CITRUS, FETA & RED ONION SALAD

- 2 blood oranges
- 1 tangelo
- 1 orange
- 1 small red onion, halved and finely sliced
- 150 g Greek feta, crumbled
- handful of rocket leaves
- large handful of mint leaves, roughly torn

DRESSING

- 2 tablespoons extra-virgin olive oil
- 1 tablespoon red wine vinegar
- 1 teaspoon honey
- pinch of Aleppo pepper
- sea salt and black pepper

This salad combines some really good things – zingy citrus, creamy feta and peppery rocket. It has only a handful of ingredients, but they all play their part in making a well-loved and versatile dish. I've suggested a combination of citrus here – blood oranges, tangelo and orange, as they not only look beautiful but bring different levels of acidity and flavour to such a simple salad. That being said, even one type of citrus, like orange, will still be wonderful.

Using a sharp knife, slice the bottoms and tops off all the citrus. Peel the citrus, starting from the top and following the curve of the flesh to the bottom. Cut the peeled citrus into 5 mm thick slices. Arrange on a plate and top with the onion, feta, rocket and mint.

Combine all the dressing ingredients in a jar and shake to emulsify. Adjust the seasoning to taste, then pour the dressing over the salad and serve.

SERVES 4

PEACHES & AVOCADO

WITH BUTTERMILK DRESSING

- 100 g baby spinach leaves (or mâche, if available)
- 3 white or yellow peaches, cut into wedges
- 1 avocado, halved and cut into 2 cm pieces
- large handful of mint leaves, roughly torn
- small handful of coriander leaves
- 1 tablespoon sesame seeds, toasted
- 40 g toasted blanched almonds

BUTTERMILK DRESSING

- 3 tablespoons buttermilk
- 2 tablespoons extra-virgin olive oil
- juice of ½ lemon
- 1 teaspoon dijon mustard
- sea salt and black pepper

I first ate mâche, often known as lamb's lettuce, on my first trip to Italy as an eighteen-year-old. I was staying on my friend's couch in Milan and as I was pretty strapped for cash, I ate a lot of salads with supermarket ingredients for lunch. Usually canned tuna, corn, buffalo mozzarella and some sort of salad leaf. I became utterly obsessed with mâche, known as songino or valerianella in Italian. It's delicate and nutty but is tricky to find here, so I have suggested baby spinach as an alternative. If you do come across some, it is really special and is great in this salad. The buttermilk gives a lovely tang and the combination of peach, avocado and sesame is just wonderful.

Place all the buttermilk dressing ingredients in a jar and shake well. Adjust the seasoning to taste and set aside.

Arrange all the salad ingredients on a serving plate and gently toss so they are somewhat layered. Pour on the dressing and serve.

SERVES 4

BRAISED LEEKS, POTATOES & PANGRATTATO

Here is a beautifully simple dish, with sweet braised leeks, soft potatoes and a crunchy thyme and lemon pangrattato. If you can find pencil leeks, they are wonderful; simply use eight rather than the six regular leeks suggested. I like to serve the pangrattato separately and allow everyone at the table to sprinkle it on for themselves, to ensure it stays nice and crunchy.

- 6 leeks
- 3 tablespoons extra-virgin olive oil
- 1 tablespoon unsalted butter
- 300 g potatoes (such as Dutch cream or nicola), peeled and cut into 2.5 cm pieces
- 2 garlic cloves, crushed
- 100 ml dry white wine
- 300 ml chicken stock
- 2 thyme sprigs
- sea salt and black pepper

PANGRATTATO

- 1 tablespoon extra-virgin olive oil
- 50 g fresh breadcrumbs
- 2 thyme sprigs, leaves picked
- finely grated zest of 1 lemon
- sea salt

Trim the leeks so you are left with the white part and very pale green part only. Halve them lengthways and sit them in cold water for 10 minutes to dislodge any sand or dirt. Pat dry.

Warm the olive oil and butter in a large frying pan over a medium heat. Add the leek and potato and cook for 3–4 minutes or until just becoming a little golden. Add the garlic and stir so that it is well distributed in the pan. Deglaze with the wine, scraping the bottom of the pan to lift any brown bits. Allow to simmer for a minute, then add the stock and thyme and season with salt and pepper.

Wet a piece of baking paper and scrunch it to soften. Unfurl the paper and place it directly on the vegetables. Reduce the heat to low and braise for 45 minutes or until the vegetables are tender and most of the liquid has evaporated.

Meanwhile, for the pangrattato, heat the olive oil in a frying pan over a medium–high heat and add the breadcrumbs. Stir to coat them in the oil and cook for 2–3 minutes or until they are golden and crunchy. Add the thyme and cook for 30 seconds, then transfer to a plate lined with paper towel to drain. Tip the breadcrumbs into a bowl, add the lemon zest and season to taste with salt.

Serve the braised vegetables topped with the pangrattato.

SERVES 4

GREEK FENNEL FRITTERS

It's a warm early spring afternoon, fennel is incredibly abundant, and we all need a snack. I make these fennel fritters; frying, eating, frying, eating. I love to serve them simply, with a lemony yoghurt beside them on the plate so the fritters can be happily dragged through. The piping-hot fritters with the cool yoghurt and a squeeze of lemon is a complete joy. A specialty of Tinos, a Greek Island in the Aegean Sea, these fritters are an absolute favourite in my house.

- 1 fennel bulb, very finely diced, fronds reserved and finely chopped
- 1 onion, very finely diced
- 2 spring onions, finely sliced
- ½ teaspoon fennel seeds, toasted and crushed
- 200 g self-raising flour
- sea salt and black pepper
- 125–150 ml cold sparkling water
- light extra-virgin olive oil or neutral vegetable oil, for frying

LEMON YOGHURT

- 200 g full-fat Greek yoghurt
- finely grated zest of 1 lemon
- 2 teaspoons extra-virgin olive oil
- sea salt

Combine the fennel, onion, spring onion and fennel seeds in a large bowl and mix well. Add the flour and season with salt and pepper. Pour in enough sparkling water to make a thick, porridge-like consistency.

Pour the olive or vegetable oil into a saucepan to a depth of 5 cm and heat to 175°C or until a little batter dropped in the oil browns in 15 seconds. Cooking in batches and using a second spoon to help, drop tablespoon amounts of the batter into the hot oil and cook the fritters for 2–3 minutes, turning halfway, until golden and cooked through. Drain the fritters on paper towel or a wire rack and season with salt.

Meanwhile, mix the lemon yoghurt ingredients together in a bowl.

Serve the fennel fritters immediately with the lemon yoghurt.

SERVES 4–6

CHARRED EGGPLANT

WITH ROASTED CHICKPEAS & LEMON

I love eggplant when it is all soft and creamy from being charred on the grill. Even better if it has been slowly cooked over charcoal, but a regular barbecue or stove is fine, too. Here, it's met with a lemony marinade and topped with gently spiced roasted chickpeas, which you could double and snack on while the eggplant is cooking. I like to create a little bed of labneh on the serving plate, but a generous dollop of plain yoghurt is also really lovely. Have some flatbread on hand to drag through the labneh and eggplant.

- 2 eggplants
- 1 lemon
- 2 garlic cloves, finely grated
- large handful of mint leaves, roughly chopped, plus extra to serve
- 2 tablespoons extra-virgin olive oil, plus extra for drizzling
- sea salt
- 200 g labneh (or homemade, see page 214)

ROASTED CHICKPEAS

- 400 g can chickpeas, drained and rinsed
- 2 tablespoons extra-virgin olive oil
- 2 teaspoons bahārāt (see page 134)
- 1 teaspoon finely grated ginger
- 1 teaspoon brown sugar
- sea salt and black pepper

Cook the eggplants, turning frequently, on a grill until blackened and collapsed. When cool enough to touch, peel away and discard the blackened skin. Transfer the flesh to a bowl. Finely grate the lemon zest, then halve the lemon, scoop out the flesh and roughly chop. Discard the pith and add the flesh and zest to the eggplant along with the garlic, mint and olive oil. Season with salt and marinate for 15–20 minutes at room temperature, or overnight in the fridge.

Preheat the oven to 180°C fan-forced. Line a baking tray with baking paper.

For the roasted chickpeas, pat dry the chickpeas and place them in a bowl, along with the olive oil, bahārāt, ginger and brown sugar. Season to taste with salt and pepper and mix to coat. Transfer to the tray and roast for 30–35 minutes or until the chickpeas are nicely coloured. Allow to cool.

Spread the labneh on a serving plate and top with the marinated eggplant and roasted chickpeas. Scatter on the extra mint and drizzle on some extra olive oil. Season to taste with salt and serve.

SERVES 4

CELERIAC & APPLE SALAD

Inspired by a classic celeriac remoulade, this lighter celeriac and apple salad is a great option in winter when you're craving something fresh. The subtle nuttiness of the celeriac and the bright tartness from the apple is such a lovely combination. I've added toasted hazelnuts here, but almonds or even some toasted pumpkin seeds or sesame seeds would also be delicious. I have added plenty of herbs as they bring a lot of flavour and colour and shouldn't be skimped on. While a traditional dressing is rather mayonnaise-heavy, I like to lean on Greek yoghurt to bring some freshness and move the dish more into salad territory. A mandoline is very helpful here, to slice the celeriac into uniformly thin matchsticks.

- 1 celeriac (about 600 g), trimmed and peeled
- 2 granny smith apples, unpeeled
- large handful each of mint leaves, parsley leaves and dill fronds, roughly chopped
- small handful of tarragon leaves, finely chopped
- 80 g hazelnuts, toasted and roughly chopped

MAYONNAISE

- 1 egg
- 2 teaspoons dijon mustard
- sea salt
- 300 ml neutral vegetable oil or light-flavoured extra-virgin olive oil or a mixture of both
- 2 teaspoons white wine vinegar or juice of ½ lemon, plus extra as needed

DRESSING

- 120 g full-fat Greek yoghurt
- 2 tablespoons white vinegar
- 2 teaspoons dijon mustard
- sea salt and black pepper

To make the mayonnaise, place the egg, mustard and a good pinch of salt in a food processor. With the motor running, very slowly add the oil in a thin stream and continue to process until the mixture is pale and thick. Add the vinegar or lemon juice and continue to process. Check for seasoning and acidity, adding more salt and vinegar or lemon, as needed. Transfer to a jar or airtight container and store in the fridge for up to a week.

Using a 3 mm tooth blade on a mandoline, cut the celeriac into matchsticks and place in a bowl of iced acidulated water. Allow to soak for 15 minutes, then drain and pat dry. Transfer to a large bowl.

Using the same blade on the mandoline, cut the apple into matchsticks and add to the bowl with the celeriac, along with the herbs and hazelnuts. Toss to combine and set aside.

Combine 120 g of the mayonnaise with the dressing ingredients in a bowl, whisk and adjust the seasoning to taste.

Pour the dressing over the salad, mix well to combine and serve.

SERVES 4

PARMIGIANA DI MELANZANE

Parmigiana di melanzane is an end of summer staple and should only really be made when eggplants are at their best. There are many theories regarding the origin of the name; the one I find most fascinating is that parmigiana originates from the word 'parmiciane', which, in old Sicilian, is the name used to describe Persian wooden shutters. A lovely image to embrace as you fry and layer each slice of eggplant in the dish.

- light extra-virgin olive oil, for frying
- 1.2 kg eggplants, cut into 4 mm thick rounds
- 4 × 100 g buffalo mozzarella balls or fior di latte, roughly torn
- 100 g Pecorino Romano, finely grated

TOMATO SUGO

- 2 tablespoons extra-virgin olive oil
- 4 garlic cloves, finely chopped
- 700 g passata
- a few basil leaves and their stalks, plus plenty of extra basil leaves to assemble
- sea salt

For the tomato sugo, gently warm the olive oil in a saucepan over a low heat. Add the garlic and cook until just softened but not coloured. Add the passata, basil and a good pinch of salt. Increase the heat to medium and cook until slightly reduced and thickened, 8–10 minutes. Set aside.

Preheat the oven to 180°C fan-forced.

Line a tray with plenty of paper towel. Heat 1–1.5 cm of olive oil in a large deep frying pan over a medium–high heat. When the oil is hot (a slice of eggplant will sizzle immediately), fry the eggplant slices in batches for 2–3 minutes or until golden on both sides. Transfer to the tray to drain.

Have all your ingredients and a lasagne or baking dish at the ready. I use a 30 cm oval copper baking dish, or 25 cm × 28 cm × 7 cm dish. Slightly smaller and the finished dish will be taller; larger and it will have fewer layers.

To assemble, spoon a thin layer of sugo over the base of your dish. Now add a layer of fried eggplant, slightly overlapping the slices, another layer of sugo, some extra basil leaves, the mozzarella or fior di latte and a good scattering of the Pecorino Romano. Repeat until you have used all the ingredients, finishing with a layer of sugo and a scattering of Pecorino Romano. Bake for 30–35 minutes or until the parmigiana is visibly bubbling. Allow to cool for at least 30 minutes, even longer is ideal. If you cut the parmigiana while it's hot, just like with lasagne, it will be incredibly sloppy.

SERVES 6–8

CHAPTER SIX

Cakes, bakes & biscuits

As well as what is in season, my cooking is guided by a memory or mood or simply by what is in my pantry.

LUNETTES

My simple sablé recipe forms the base for these gorgeous French biscuits. Lunettes translates to 'glasses' or 'spectacles', and while they don't need to be this exact shape, they do look lovely. I make a straightforward raspberry jam, flavoured with a little basil, which brings a subtle herbaceousness to the finished biscuits. Any good-quality, store-bought jam will work well, too.

- 250 g (1⅔ cups) plain flour
- 150 g cold unsalted butter, cubed
- 80 g caster sugar
- pinch of sea salt
- 1 teaspoon vanilla extract or vanilla bean paste
- 1 egg
- pure icing sugar, sifted, to serve

RASPBERRY JAM

- 400 g raspberries
- 300 g caster sugar
- 2 basil sprigs
- juice of ½ lemon

For the raspberry jam, mash the raspberries and caster sugar together in a saucepan. Add the basil and stir well until the sugar has dissolved. Bring to the boil over a medium–high heat, skimming any foam that rises to the surface. Add the lemon juice and continue to cook until the jam reaches 103–104°C on an instant-read thermometer. Ladle the jam into a warm sterilised jar, seal and allow to cool. Due to the jam's low sugar percentage (usually jam has a 1:1 ratio of fruit to sugar), this jam should be stored in the fridge and used within a week.

Place the flour, butter, caster sugar and salt in a food processor and pulse to a fine crumb. Add the vanilla and egg and continue to pulse until the dough begins to look damp and is coming together. Turn out onto a clean work surface and shape into a disc. Wrap in plastic wrap or baking paper and refrigerate for 30 minutes.

Line two baking trays with baking paper.

Roll the dough out between two pieces of baking paper until 3–4 mm thick. Cut out the biscuits using a fluted almond-shaped cutter about 10 cm in size. Reroll the scraps and cut out more biscuits, so you have 24 in total. Use a 2 cm round cutter (I use a piping bag tip) to cut two rounds in half of the biscuits (to make the 'lunettes'). Transfer the biscuits to the trays and refrigerate for 30 minutes.

Preheat the oven to 180°C fan-forced.

Bake the biscuits for 10–12 minutes or until lightly golden. Allow to cool.

Spread the jam on the biscuit bases without holes and top each with a cut out 'lunette' biscuit, sandwiching the jam between the biscuit layers. Dust with the icing sugar and serve.

MAKES 12

MADELEINES

WITH ORANGE SUGAR

There are few things more special than a still-warm madeleine straight from the oven. Here, rolled in an orange sugar, they are perfect in their simplicity and really don't need much else. When in season, I love to use blood oranges instead. You could also simply dust them with icing sugar. My kids love these with a glass of cold milk, and, truthfully, so do I.

The batter really does require the rest in the fridge, and while I think it is optimal for them to rest for just 45–60 minutes, they are still wonderful if rested overnight and made the next day.

- 3 eggs
- 80 g (⅓ cup) caster sugar
- 40 g honey
- finely grated zest of 1 orange
- 1 teaspoon orange-blossom water
- 1 teaspoon vanilla extract or vanilla bean paste
- 150 g self-raising flour
- good pinch of sea salt
- 150 g unsalted butter, melted and cooled, plus extra for greasing

ORANGE SUGAR

- finely grated zest of 1 orange
- 80 g caster sugar

Place the eggs, caster sugar and honey in the bowl of a stand mixer fitted with the whisk attachment and whisk for 8–10 minutes or until very voluminous and pale. Whisk in the orange zest, orange-blossom water and vanilla. Gently fold in the flour and salt, being very careful not to overmix, then fold in the melted butter. Cover and refrigerate the batter for 45–60 minutes.

To make the orange sugar, place the orange zest and sugar in a small bowl and rub the zest into the sugar until damp and fragrant. Set aside.

Preheat the oven to 180°C fan-forced.

Brush a madeleine tin with the extra melted butter, then spoon about 1 tablespoon of the batter into each madeleine mould. Bake for 10–12 minutes or until the madeleines are golden and risen. Remove the madeleines from the tin, roll in the orange sugar and eat warm.

MAKES 18

CINNAMON SUGAR BUNS

This is something I make for a special breakfast or morning tea. The dough is a flaky laminated brioche called 'brioche feuilletée' and does require a little folding, rolling and turning to create the buttery layers of the bun. For a little citrus twist, you can add some orange or lemon zest to either the cinnamon sugar or the sugar the buns are rolled in. These buns are best eaten the day they are made.

melted butter, for brushing

LAMINATED BRIOCHE

- 400 g tipo 0 flour, plus extra for dusting
- 45 g caster sugar
- 5 g active dried yeast
- 5 g fine sea salt
- 3 eggs
- 100 ml full-cream milk
- 125 g unsalted butter, softened, plus extra for greasing

BUTTER BLOCK

- 150 g unsalted butter, chilled but not firm

CINNAMON SUGAR FILLING

- 100 g caster sugar, plus extra for dusting and rolling
- 50 g brown sugar
- 2 tablespoons ground cinnamon
- pinch of sea salt

CINNAMON SUGAR DUSTING

- 60 g caster sugar
- 2 teaspoons ground cinnamon

Place the laminated brioche ingredients in the bowl of a stand mixer fitted with the dough hook attachment and mix on a medium speed to combine. Reduce the speed to medium–low and mix for 15–18 minutes or until the dough is strong and elastic. To check whether enough gluten has developed in the dough, stop the mixer and pull out a little piece of the dough. With both your hands, stretch it out. It should stretch without tearing until almost transparent. This is called the 'windowpane method'. Continue mixing and checking until you can create the 'windowpane' successfully.

Turn the dough out onto a clean work surface and shape into a ball. Transfer to a lightly greased bowl, cover with plastic wrap and refrigerate for 12–24 hours.

For the butter block, place the butter between two pieces of baking paper and roll into a rough rectangular shape, about 5 mm thick. Place on a tray and refrigerate for 30 minutes.

Turn the dough out onto a lightly floured work surface and roll out to form a 1.5 cm thick rectangle. Place the butter block in the centre of the dough and fold the dough from the shortest ends into the middle to meet, pressing to seal in the butter. Roll out the dough to form a 1 cm thick rectangle, then rotate it 90 degrees and repeat the folding, rolling and rotating three more times. In total, you should have folded the dough four times. Wrap the dough in plastic wrap or baking paper and refrigerate for 2 hours.

Meanwhile, combine the cinnamon sugar filling ingredients in a small bowl.

Grease a 12-hole cupcake tin with melted butter and dust with some extra caster sugar.

Roll the dough into a rectangle, approximately 48 cm × 30 cm in size and around 5 mm thick. Sprinkle evenly with the cinnamon sugar filling.

Trim the ends on the shortest sides to create straight edges, then cut the dough into twelve 4 cm wide strips. Roll the strips into snails and nestle them in the tin, spiral-side up. Cover loosely with a tea towel and allow to rise in a warm place for 2 hours or until doubled in size.

Preheat the oven to 200°C fan-forced.

Place the buns in the oven, immediately reduce the temperature to 180°C fan-forced and bake for 18–20 minutes or until risen and golden. Let the buns cool in the tin for 8–10 minutes, then transfer to a wire rack and allow to cool completely.

Combine the cinnamon sugar dusting ingredients in a tray. Roll the cooled buns in the cinnamon sugar and serve.

MAKES 12

OLIVE OIL LOAF CAKE

WITH PEAR & HAZELNUT

Pears are such a gift in late autumn and throughout winter. They are wonderful poached and served with custard or cooked in caramel for a tarte tatin. Admittedly, they are often the fruit left to get a little too soft in our fruit bowl, so I do tend to bake with them more often than not. Here, they are poached in a light syrup spiked with star anise and vanilla. The tender pieces of pear, almost jewel-like, are folded through the hazelnut and olive oil cake batter while the syrup is poured onto the hot cake straight from the oven – a pure delight.

- 3 eggs
- 150 g caster sugar
- finely grated zest of 1 lemon
- 100 ml light-flavoured extra-virgin olive oil, plus extra to serve
- 120 g ground hazelnuts
- 125 g self-raising flour
- good pinch of sea salt
- crème fraîche, to serve

POACHED PEARS

- 100 g caster sugar
- 1 star anise
- 1 vanilla pod, split and seeds scraped
- juice of ½ lemon
- 2 firm pears, peeled, cored and cut into 2 cm pieces

Preheat the oven to 180°C fan-forced. Grease and line a 23 cm × 12 cm loaf tin.

For the poached pears, place the caster sugar, star anise, vanilla pod and seeds, 250 ml (1 cup) of water and the lemon juice in a small saucepan. Bring to a simmer over a medium heat, then add the pears and cook for 6–8 minutes or until just tender. Remove the pears with a slotted spoon and set aside. If the syrup lacks viscosity, continue to simmer the syrup until slightly thickened, remembering it will thicken upon cooling. Reserve the syrup for later.

Whisk together the eggs, caster sugar and lemon zest in a large bowl. Stream in the olive oil and whisk until just incorporated. Whisk in the ground hazelnuts, then finally whisk in the flour and salt until just combined. Fold in the pears and spoon the batter into the tin. Bake for 45–50 minutes or until a skewer comes out clean when tested. Use a toothpick to poke holes in the hot cake, then pour on the cooled syrup. Allow the cake to cool in the tin, then turn out and serve with the crème fraîche and a drizzle of olive oil.

SERVES 8

ALMOND CRUMBLE CAKE

WITH PEACH & BLACKBERRY

The magnificent combination of peaches and blackberries is one I never tire of. I love the contrast in colour, but also the sweetness of the peaches alongside the slightly tart blackberries. Here, they form the middle layer of a cake gently spiced with cloves and topped with an almond crumble. You could swap the almonds for hazelnuts in both the cake and crumble, something I often do. I love the generosity of this cake, both in its layers and in its size. It's perfect for an afternoon crowd or a summer's picnic.

- 200 g unsalted butter, softened
- 150 g caster sugar
- 100 g brown sugar
- 3 eggs
- 150 ml full-cream milk
- 100 g (1 cup) almond meal
- 200 g self-raising flour
- ½ teaspoon ground cloves
- pinch of sea salt
- pure icing sugar, to dust

ALMOND CRUMBLE

- 60 g (⅔ cup) flaked almonds
- 60 g plain flour
- 50 g caster sugar
- 40 g almond meal
- pinch of sea salt
- 60 g cold unsalted butter, cubed

FRUIT FILLING

- 4 yellow peaches (around 550 g)
- 20 g caster sugar
- ½ teaspoon ground cinnamon
- 2 teaspoons plain flour
- 125 g blackberries, halved

Preheat the oven to 180°C fan-forced. Grease and line a 30 cm × 20 cm × 5 cm rectangular baking tin.

Combine the almond crumble ingredients in a bowl. Rub the butter into the dry ingredients until the mixture is damp and holds together in a crumbly manner. Set aside.

For the fruit filling, make a cross in the base of each peach, blanch in boiling water for 1–2 minutes, then transfer to an ice bath. Peel off the skin and discard. Cut the peaches into wedges and place in a bowl with the caster sugar, cinnamon and flour. Toss to coat and set aside.

Cream the butter and sugars in the large bowl of a stand mixer fitted with the paddle attachment on a medium–high speed for 6–8 minutes or until pale and very fluffy. Add the eggs, one at a time, beating well after each addition and scraping down the bowl with a spatula as needed. Add the milk and mix until combined. The mixture may look curdled at this stage, but it will come together. Reduce the speed to low and add the almond meal, flour, ground cloves and salt and mix until just combined.

Spoon the batter into the tin and smooth the surface with the spatula. Arrange the peaches evenly on the batter, then top with the blackberries. Scatter on the almond crumble and bake for 45–50 minutes or until the top springs back when touched. Allow to cool in the tin for 15 minutes, then transfer to a wire rack to cool completely. Dust with icing sugar and serve.

SERVES 8–10

BANANA & CARDAMOM LOAF

A very simple and comforting loaf cake that I often make with overripe bananas. The crunchy sugar crust contrasts with the soft fragrant interior and is especially good eaten warm with some salted butter. Ideally, the cardamom should be freshly ground, as its flavour is much more pronounced. Simply pound some whole cardamom pods using a mortar and pestle, discard the papery pods and continue to grind the seeds.

- demerara sugar, for sprinkling
- 150 g caster sugar
- 100 g brown sugar
- 3 eggs
- 2 ripe bananas (around 200 g peeled), mashed
- 1 teaspoon vanilla extract or vanilla bean paste
- 200 g unsalted butter, melted and cooled
- 250 g (1⅔ cups) self-raising flour
- 1 teaspoon ground cardamom
- pinch of sea salt

Preheat the oven to 180°C fan-forced. Grease a 23 cm × 12 cm loaf tin, then sprinkle in some demerara sugar, shake the tin to coat the base and sides and tap out the excess.

Beat the caster sugar and brown sugar with the eggs in the bowl of a stand mixer fitted with the paddle attachment on a medium–high speed until very pale and thick (around 5–6 minutes). Reduce the speed of the mixer to low, add the banana and vanilla and beat to incorporate. Pour in the melted butter and beat to combine. Add the flour, cardamom and salt, then mix until just combined.

Spoon the batter into the tin and sprinkle some demerara sugar over the top of the cake. Bake for 45–50 minutes or until a skewer comes out clean when tested. Allow the cake to cool in the tin for 15 minutes, then transfer to a wire rack to cool completely.

SERVES 8

SOUR CHERRY RICOTTA CAKE

Inspired by a sour cherry and ricotta tart I ate in Rome, this cake is light, fluffy and a wonderful combination of sweet and tart. Sour cherries, such as Morello and Amarena, are complex in flavour and usually only used for preserving in syrup for cakes and desserts. If you're lucky enough to find a cherry farm that grows sour cherries, usually later in the season, they are a real treat. You can also find them frozen at many grocers and supermarkets; these are what I suggest you use for this upside-down sour cherry cake. If you can't source them, I have also made this cake with frozen blueberries, which work very well, too.

- 500 g frozen sour cherries
- 80 g (⅓ cup) caster sugar
- 40 g unsalted butter
- juice of ½ lemon

CAKE

- 250 g caster sugar
- 3 eggs
- finely grated zest of 1 lemon
- 2 teaspoons vanilla extract or vanilla bean paste
- 150 ml light-flavoured extra-virgin olive oil
- 250 g fresh full-fat ricotta, plus extra to serve
- 250 g (1⅔ cups) self-raising flour
- ½ teaspoon freshly grated nutmeg
- pinch of sea salt

Preheat the oven to 180°C fan-forced. Grease and line a 23 cm round cake tin.

Combine the cherries, caster sugar, butter and lemon juice in a saucepan and cook over a medium heat for 8–10 minutes or until the syrup has thickened a little and the cherries have just begun to collapse. Pour over the base of the tin and allow to cool.

For the cake, place the caster sugar, eggs, lemon zest and vanilla in a large bowl and whisk until well combined. Add the olive oil, followed by the ricotta and whisk until smooth. Finally, whisk in the flour, nutmeg and salt until just combined. Pour the batter into the tin, smooth the surface and bake for 50–55 minutes or until a skewer comes out clean when tested. Allow the cake to cool in the tin for 20 minutes, then invert the cake onto a wire rack to cool completely. Transfer to a serving plate, remove the baking paper and serve with extra ricotta.

SERVES 8–12

SPICED DATE LOAF

With a deep and rich caramel flavour and heady with spices, this loaf cake is nostalgic and comforting. I like to eat slices of it warm, slathered with salted butter. Other spices like cardamom and allspice are pleasing, too, just don't cut back on the ginger, which gives the cake its warmth. The buttermilk really does wonders here to lift and lighten, but if you don't have any, some plain full-fat yoghurt works well. I like to use medjool dates, but since they are mashed into a pulp, any date you prefer will work.

- 150 g pitted medjool dates
- ½ teaspoon bicarbonate of soda
- 80 ml (⅓ cup) boiling water
- 3 eggs
- 100 g dark muscovado sugar
- 60 g caster sugar
- 100 ml buttermilk
- 100 ml light-flavoured extra-virgin olive oil or neutral vegetable oil
- 250 g (1⅔ cups) self-raising flour
- 1 teaspoon ground ginger
- ½ teaspoon ground cinnamon
- ½ teaspoon ground nutmeg
- pinch of sea salt
- salted butter, to serve

Preheat the oven to 180°C fan-forced. Grease and line a 23 cm × 12 cm loaf tin.

Place the dates and bicarbonate of soda in a heatproof bowl and cover with the boiling water. Allow to sit for 10 minutes, then mash well with a fork.

Place the eggs and sugars in the bowl of a stand mixer fitted with the paddle attachment and beat on a high speed for 4–5 minutes or until pale and voluminous. Reduce the speed to medium and add the buttermilk, oil and mashed dates. Mix well, then reduce the speed to low, add the dry ingredients and mix until just combined.

Scrape the batter into the tin and bake for 45–50 minutes or until a skewer comes out almost clean when tested (a few crumbs are fine). Allow to cool in the tin for 15 minutes, then transfer to a wire rack to cool completely.

Serve the loaf, sliced, with the salted butter.

SERVES 8–12

BROWN BUTTER STRAWBERRY CAKE

Spring is always filled with so much anticipation. As we emerge from winter, the days become a little longer and new produce begins to appear at the markets. An abundance of berries heralds in the change and I often get a little too excited, buying far too many to eat just on their own. This cake makes wonderful use of strawberries, especially if they are not looking their best. The brown butter brings a nutty, almost caramel-like flavour to the cake, and the sugar-lined tin, while not obligatory, certainly gives a great texture. Blueberries, blackberries and raspberries can all be used in place of strawberries.

- 150 g unsalted butter, plus extra for greasing
- demerara sugar, for sprinkling
- 3 eggs
- 200 g caster sugar
- 2 teaspoons vanilla extract or vanilla bean paste
- 200 g full-fat plain yoghurt
- 100 g (1 cup) almond meal
- 200 g self-raising flour
- ½ teaspoon ground cinnamon
- good pinch of sea salt
- 250 g strawberries, hulled and halved

Preheat the oven to 180°C fan-forced. Grease a 23 cm round cake tin with butter and sprinkle in some demerara sugar, then shake the tin to coat the base and side and tap out the excess. Set aside.

Melt the butter in a small saucepan over a medium heat and simmer gently until the butter is fragrant and nut brown. Set aside to cool.

Beat the eggs and sugar in the large bowl of a stand mixer fitted with the paddle attachment on a high speed for 7–8 minutes or until pale and voluminous. Add the vanilla and yoghurt and beat to combine. Reduce the speed to low and add the almond meal, flour, cinnamon and salt. Mix until just combined. Pour in the cooled browned butter and mix until just incorporated.

Spoon the batter into the tin and smooth the surface. Arrange the halved strawberries, cut-side up, on top of the cake batter. Sprinkle on some demerara sugar and bake for 50–55 minutes or until a skewer comes out clean when tested. Allow to cool in the tin for 15 minutes, then transfer to a wire rack to cool completely.

SERVES 8–12

PISTACHIO SAFFRON CAKE

WITH LEMON SAFFRON ICING

I have a real love for simple cakes, ones that can be made with just a bowl and whisk, and when they are topped with a glossy zingy icing, all the better. The saffron in this cake imbues a floral and earthy note that pairs so well with the pistachios. Grinding the saffron up with a pinch of sugar ensures it permeates the whole cake.

- pinch of saffron threads
- 200 g caster sugar
- 3 eggs
- 100 ml light-flavoured extra-virgin olive oil
- 150 g full-fat Greek yoghurt
- finely grated zest of 1 lemon
- 150 g ground pistachios
- 50 g almond meal
- 150 g (1 cup) self-raising flour
- good pinch of sea salt
- 60 g pistachios, roughly chopped
- labneh (or homemade, see page 214), to serve

LEMON SAFFRON ICING

- pinch of saffron threads
- juice of 1 lemon, plus extra as needed
- 125 g (1 cup) pure icing sugar, plus extra as needed

Preheat the oven to 180°C fan-forced. Grease and line a 21 cm round cake tin.

Using a mortar and pestle, pound the saffron with 2 teaspoons of the caster sugar to a fine powder. Place in a large bowl, along with the remaining caster sugar and the eggs, and whisk until very well combined. Pour in the olive oil and whisk until incorporated, then whisk in the yoghurt and lemon zest. Mix in the ground pistachios and almond meal, then fold in the flour and salt, being careful not to overmix.

Pour the batter into the tin and bake for 40–45 minutes or until a skewer comes out clean when tested. Allow the cake to cool in the tin for 15 minutes, then transfer to a wire rack to cool completely.

For the lemon saffron icing, place the saffron in a small saucepan and pour on the lemon juice. Gently warm over a medium heat, then allow to cool. Sift the icing sugar into a large bowl and pour on the saffron-infused lemon juice. Whisk to create a smooth and thick icing. If too runny, sift in more icing sugar; if too thick, add some more lemon juice.

Pour the icing onto the cooled cake and top with the pistachios. Allow to set, then serve the cake, sliced, with a dollop of labneh.

SERVES 8–12

TORTA PARADISO

A beautiful Italian butter cake, with a texture so light and divine it's no wonder its name means paradise. Often split and filled with strawberries and cream, I instead serve it simply with a dollop of crème fraîche, ricotta or mascarpone and seasonal fruit; macerated berries, stewed rhubarb (see page 217) or, as here, with some stewed plums. Even a spoonful of Amarena cherries in syrup is lovely. It is also completely acceptable and very traditional to serve it as is, dusted with icing sugar.

Originally created by Pavese pastry chef Enrico Vigoni in the late 1800s, torta paradiso is still on the menu at Vigoni and celebrated across Italy, especially in Lombardy, for its simplicity and lightness.

- 250 g unsalted butter, softened
- 250 g caster sugar
- 4 eggs
- finely grated zest of 1 lemon
- 125 g self-raising flour
- 125 g potato starch
- good pinch of sea salt
- pure icing sugar, sifted, for dusting
- crème fraîche, fresh full-fat ricotta or mascarpone, to serve

STEWED PLUMS

- 100 g caster sugar
- 1 vanilla pod, split and seeds scraped
- 3 strips of lemon peel
- juice of 1 lemon
- 1 fresh bay leaf
- 600 g plums, halved and stones removed

Preheat the oven to 180°C fan-forced. Grease and line a 23 cm round cake tin.

Cream the butter and sugar in the large bowl of a stand mixer fitted with the paddle attachment on a medium–high speed for 6–8 minutes or until pale and very fluffy. Scrape down the bowl with a spatula intermittently if needed. Reduce the speed to medium and add the eggs, one at a time, beating well after each addition. Add the lemon zest and mix to combine.

Remove the bowl from the stand mixer and sift in the flour, potato starch and salt. Gently fold into the mixture with the spatula until just combined, being careful not to overmix. The batter will be quite stiff.

Transfer the batter to the tin and bake for 45–50 minutes or until a skewer comes out clean when tested. Allow the cake to cool in the tin for 15 minutes, then remove from the tin and transfer to a wire rack cool completely.

For the stewed plums, place the caster sugar, vanilla pod and seeds, lemon peel, lemon juice and bay leaf in a large saucepan and add 200 ml of water. Bring to a simmer over a high heat and cook for 6–8 minutes or until the syrup is slightly thickened. Add the plums and reduce the heat to medium–low. Gently stew the plums for 10–12 minutes or until they begin to collapse. Very ripe plums will take no time at all, so be sure to keep a close eye on them.

Dust the cake with the icing sugar and serve with the crème fraîche, ricotta or mascarpone and the stewed plums.

SERVES 8–12

CHAPTER SEVEN

Sweets to finish

PAGES 208–227

Even if a dish or meal is thrown together at the last minute, it should always feel intentional.

PORTOKALOPITA

Growing up, our Greek neighbours would bring over large squares of portokalopita. I adored its light spongy texture and the sweet orange syrup it was bathed in. It wasn't until I was an adult that I realised just how ingenious the recipe is. Filo sheets, torn into pieces and dried out, are mixed with an orange, yoghurt and olive oil mixture before being baked, then drenched in syrup. The result is a cross between a cake and a pudding – perfect for dessert with coffee. I sometimes use blood orange or tangelo instead of the traditional orange, but here I keep it pretty classic. Portokalopita is even better the following day, once the syrup has had a really good chance to soak in.

- 500 g filo pastry
- 1 orange
- 180 g caster sugar
- 3 eggs
- 200 g full-fat Greek yoghurt, plus extra to serve
- 150 ml light-flavoured extra-virgin olive oil, plus extra for greasing
- 2 teaspoons vanilla extract or vanilla bean paste
- ½ teaspoon baking powder
- pinch of ground cinnamon

ORANGE SYRUP

- juice of 1 orange
- 2 strips of orange peel
- 150 g caster sugar
- 1 cinnamon stick
- 2 cloves

Using your hands, tear the filo pastry into smallish pieces. Lay them out on a tray and allow them to dry out for at least 1½ hours, but overnight is great, too.

Place the orange in a saucepan and cover with water. Bring to the boil and cook for 35–40 minutes or until the orange is soft. Allow to cool, then halve it, remove any seeds and roughly chop. Place the chopped orange in a food processor or blender, add the caster sugar, eggs, yoghurt, olive oil, vanilla, baking powder and cinnamon and blitz until smooth.

Preheat the oven to 180°C fan-forced. Grease a 24 cm square cake tin with a little olive oil.

Place the dried filo pastry in the tin and pour on the orange mixture. Mix well with a fork, coating all the pastry without pressing down too much. Bake for 35–40 minutes or until the portokalopita is lightly risen and golden.

While the portokalopita is cooking, combine the orange syrup ingredients with 200 ml of water in a saucepan over a high heat. Stir to dissolve the sugar, then bring to the boil. Reduce the heat to medium and simmer for 6–8 minutes or until syrupy. Allow to cool.

When the hot portokalopita comes out of the oven, pour over the cooled syrup, including the cinnamon stick and cloves. Allow to cool in the tin. Serve the portokalopita with the extra yoghurt.

SERVES 8–12

ROAST APRICOTS

WITH LABNEH & SESAME BRITTLE

Roasting stone fruit is a great way to intensify or improve their flavour. Apricots are a particular favourite of mine to roast as they are slightly tart and can often be improved with a little sugar and time in the oven or on the stove. I like to eat roasted stone fruit with yoghurt or labneh, and topped with something for crunch. Some toasted nuts, granola or, as I suggest here, a sesame brittle that is nutty and sweet. You can buy labneh that has already been hung, but making it yourself really is very easy and a great thing to know how to do.

- 1 kg apricots, halved and stones removed
- 120 g raw sugar
- 160 ml white wine
- juice of 1 lemon
- 3 cardamom pods, bruised
- 1 cinnamon stick

LABNEH

- 1 kg full-fat Greek yoghurt

SESAME BRITTLE

- 60 g caster sugar
- 50 g toasted white sesame seeds

To make the labneh, the night before you want to serve, place the yoghurt in a strainer lined with a clean piece of muslin and set the strainer over a bowl. Place the yoghurt in the fridge and let it drain overnight. (The whey that collects in the bowl can be reserved for other uses, such as adding to smoothies or drinks.)

Preheat the oven to 190°C fan-forced.

Arrange the apricot halves, cut-side up, in a baking dish so they fit snugly. Sprinkle on the raw sugar, then pour the white wine and lemon juice around the dish. Nestle in the cardamom pods and cinnamon stick and roast, basting the apricots halfway through, for 40–45 minutes or until the apricots are just beginning to collapse and the syrup has reduced. The cooking time will depend on the ripeness of the fruit.

While the apricots are roasting, make the sesame brittle. Line a baking tray with baking paper. Combine the caster sugar and 1 tablespoon of water in a small saucepan. Place over a medium–high heat and bring to a simmer, swirling the pan as needed to dissolve the sugar. Any sugar crystallising on the side of the pan can be brushed down with a pastry brush dipped in water. Once the caramel has turned a deep amber, tip in the sesame seeds, immediately stir to coat the seeds in the caramel, then pour onto the prepared tray. Place another sheet of baking paper on the sesame caramel and roll out using a rolling pin to make it as thin as possible. Allow to cool, then remove the paper. Break the brittle into shards and set aside.

Make a bed of labneh on a serving plate, top with the roasted apricots, their roasting juices and the sesame brittle shards and serve. Any leftover labneh can be transferred to an airtight container and stored in the fridge for up to 10 days.

SERVES 6–8

CREAMY RICE PUDDING

WITH RHUBARB, RASPBERRIES & CARDAMOM

A comforting dessert that can be varied depending on what fruit is in season, I love it with rhubarb as the sharpness cuts through the creaminess really well. I like to add fresh bay leaf and lemon peel to my rice pudding – they imbue some brightness and interest in a harmonious way. Orange peel works well, too. Depending on the season, stewed apricots or plums are also lovely stirred through the pudding. If you want to eat the pudding cold, simply loosen with some milk or cream upon serving.

- 200 g Carnaroli rice or other risotto rice
- 1 fresh bay leaf
- 1 vanilla pod, split and seeds scraped
- 3 strips of lemon peel
- 80 g (⅓ cup) caster sugar
- 1.2 litres full-cream milk, plus extra as needed
- 200 ml pure cream

STEWED RHUBARB

- 250 g rhubarb, roughly chopped
- 100 g caster sugar
- 3 cardamom pods, bruised
- juice of ½ lemon
- 125 g raspberries

To make the stewed rhubarb, place the rhubarb and sugar in a saucepan, then add the cardamom pods and 2 tablespoons of water. Stir to dissolve the sugar and cook over a medium–low heat for 8–10 minutes or until the rhubarb is soft. Stir in the lemon juice and set aside. Once cool, stir through the raspberries and set aside.

Combine the rice, bay leaf, vanilla pod and seeds, lemon peel, sugar, milk and cream in a large saucepan and stir well. Bring to a simmer over a medium heat, then reduce the heat to low and cook gently, stirring often, for 45 minutes or until the rice is al dente. If the rice begins to dry out before it is cooked, add more milk, as needed. If the rice is cooked but the pudding is a little too runny for your liking, simply allow the pudding to sit for 10–15 minutes and it will thicken upon cooling.

Remove the lemon peel, vanilla pod and bay leaf, and spoon the warm rice pudding into bowls. Top with a dollop of the stewed rhubarb and serve.

SERVES 4

APRICOT TART

Inspired by Lulu Peyraud's apricot tart in Richard Olney's *Lulu's Provençal Table*, this tart is really an uncomplicated beauty. The apricots are left to macerate in vanilla and sugar and then cooked down to an almost jam-like consistency. The result is a rich and intense apricot flavour that makes use of a glut of apricots, one of the spoils of early summer. Lulu's tart adds some sliced fresh green almonds; however, I like the silky texture of the apricots to shine, so I keep mine very simple. The pastry needs to be handled gently and care taken when rubbing in the butter, to ensure the pastry base for the apricots is flaky and tender.

- 800 g ripe apricots, halved and stones removed
- 1 vanilla pod, split and seeds scraped
- 150 g caster sugar, plus extra as needed
- 1 egg, for egg wash
- demerara sugar, for sprinkling
- crème fraîche, to serve

FLAKY PASTRY

- 250 g (1⅔ cups) plain flour, plus extra for dusting
- 1 tablespoon caster sugar
- good pinch of sea salt
- 125 g cold unsalted butter, cubed
- 1 teaspoon white vinegar
- iced water

Place the apricots and vanilla pod and seeds in a saucepan, sprinkle on the caster sugar and mix to coat. Allow to sit for 2–3 hours (up to overnight) to draw out the liquid. Set over a medium heat and cook for 12–15 minutes or until most of the liquid has evaporated, the apricots have collapsed and the temperature reaches 100–101°C on an instant-read thermometer. Allow to completely cool, then remove the vanilla pod.

For the flaky pastry, mix the flour, sugar and salt in a large bowl. Use your fingertips to rub the butter into the flour to create flat pieces of butter coated by the flour. For a flaky dough, it is important not to overwork the butter. Drizzle in the vinegar and enough iced water to just bring the dough together (you might not need all of it). It will still be shaggy, but should hold together when pressed. If there are dry or floury spots, sprinkle in a little more water, a teaspoon at a time, until the dough just comes together. Flatten into a thick disc about 10–12 cm in diameter, wrap in plastic wrap or baking paper and refrigerate for at least 1 hour.

Preheat the oven to 200°C fan-forced. Line a 30 cm round baking tray with baking paper.

Remove the pastry from the fridge and let it sit at room temperature for 10 minutes to make it easier to roll. Roll out the dough on a lightly floured work surface to form a large disc 2–3 mm thick, massaging the edges as you roll to prevent it from cracking too much. Drape the pastry over the tray.

Spread the jammy apricots over the pastry base, leaving a 3 cm border, then crimp and fold in the pastry border to form a galette.

Whisk the egg with 1 teaspoon of water, then brush the egg wash over the pastry edge. Scatter the demerara sugar over the pastry edge and bake the tart for 30–35 minutes or until the pastry is golden and the apricots are a little darker in colour. Allow to cool, then eat warm or at room temperature with some crème fraîche.

SERVES 8–12

RICOTTA STRACCIATELLA GELATO

Good-quality ricotta is important here – it should be sweet and milky and firm, but not at all dry or crumbly. If you can find some, buffalo ricotta is heavenly. Stracciatella means 'little rags' in Italian and is the name for cream-laden mozzarella strands, as well as a Roman egg broth and a gelato that has shards of chocolate rippled throughout. Created in 1961 at La Marianna in Bergamo by Enrico Panattoni and inspired by stracciatella the soup, a new gelato flavour was born. The warm melted chocolate, once it hits the cold gelato, forms shards that create a texture unlike anything else. Here, I've also added ricotta and pistachios. I love to make this for Easter or Christmas, as it feels very celebratory. Sometimes I include chopped candied fruit like cedro or clementine, too.

- 400 ml full-cream milk
- 200 ml pure cream
- 4 egg yolks
- 150 g caster sugar
- 150 g fresh full-fat ricotta
- 60 g chocolate (55–65% cocoa solids), roughly chopped
- 50 g pistachios, roughly chopped

Warm the milk and cream in a saucepan over a medium–high heat until just about to simmer.

Meanwhile, whisk the egg yolks and caster sugar in a large bowl until pale and well combined. Pour in a little of the warm milk mixture and whisk to combine. Continue pouring in the milk mixture and whisking until all is combined. Return the mixture to the same pan and cook over a medium–low heat until the custard is thick and coats the back of a wooden spoon (or until it reaches around 82°C on an instant-read thermometer). Whisk in the ricotta, then transfer to a container, cover and refrigerate overnight.

Use a stick blender or transfer the ricotta mixture to a blender and blitz until smooth. Transfer to an ice-cream machine and churn according to the manufacturer's instructions until the ice cream is the consistency of a soft serve.

Meanwhile, chill a container with a lid in the freezer.

Melt the chocolate in a small heatproof bowl set over a saucepan of barely simmering water. In the final few minutes of churning, drizzle the chocolate onto the ice cream, then add the pistachios.

Transfer the ice cream to the chilled container and cover directly with a piece of baking paper, then the lid. Freeze for 3–4 hours or until firm, then serve. The gelato is best eaten within 2 days of being made.

SERVES 8

BOUGATSA

Greek custard pies really have my heart and bougatsa is one of my favourites. A semolina custard is enveloped by flaky filo pastry and topped with icing sugar and cinnamon. Traditionally eaten for breakfast, it is also a delightful dessert and is still fantastic the day after, eaten cold straight from the fridge.

- unsalted butter, melted, for brushing
- 12 filo sheets
- pure icing sugar, sifted, for dusting
- ground cinnamon, for dusting

SEMOLINA CUSTARD

- 1.2 litres full-cream milk
- 1 vanilla pod, split and seeds scraped
- 1 cinnamon stick
- 3 strips of lemon peel
- 80 g unsalted butter, cubed
- 150 g caster sugar
- 120 g semolina
- 2 egg yolks

Preheat the oven to 180°C fan-forced. Brush a 30 cm × 25 cm × 5 cm baking tin with melted butter. Set aside.

To make the semolina custard, place the milk, vanilla pod and seeds, cinnamon stick and lemon peel in a large saucepan and warm over a medium heat, until just about to simmer. Add the butter and melt, then whisk in the caster sugar and cook, stirring frequently, until dissolved. Remove the vanilla pod and cinnamon stick and reduce the heat to low. Rain in the semolina and cook, whisking continuously, for 3–4 minutes or until the mixture has thickened. Remove from the heat and whisk in the egg yolks. Set aside.

Brush one sheet of the filo pastry with the melted butter and drape over the base of the tin. Repeat with 5 more sheets of pastry. Spoon in the semolina custard and smooth the surface. Brush one of the remaining filo sheets with some melted butter and drape over the custard. Repeat with the remaining filo sheets, loosely draping them on top and creating some ruffled textures as you lay them down. Bake for 40–45 minutes or until the filo is golden. Allow to cool. Dust with the icing sugar and cinnamon, then cut into large squares and serve.

SERVES 12

CROSTOLI

WITH MASCARPONE & BLUEBERRY COMPOTE

Crostoli go by many names in Italy, depending on the region – chiacchiere, bugie, cenci and frappe, just to name a few. In Malta, they are called xkunvat and are flavoured with anise and orange-blossom water. Often eaten during Carnevale, these fried pieces of light and airy dough are dusted with copious amounts of icing sugar. They are glorious on their own with coffee, but served with a dollop of mascarpone and this blueberry compote they become an elegant dessert. The crostoli recipe makes around 40 pieces, so more than enough for people to have a few pieces each with some left over.

- neutral vegetable oil or light-flavoured extra-virgin olive oil, for frying
- pure icing sugar, sifted, for dusting
- mascarpone, to serve

CROSTOLI

- 280 g tipo 00 flour
- 40 g caster sugar
- pinch of sea salt
- 20 g unsalted butter, softened
- 2 tablespoons rum, marsala or grappa
- finely grated zest of 1 lemon
- 1 egg
- 1 egg yolk

BLUEBERRY COMPOTE

- 350 g blueberries
- 100 caster sugar
- 1 rosemary sprig
- finely grated zest and juice of 1 lemon

For the crostoli, mix the flour, caster sugar and salt in a bowl. Add the butter and rub it into the flour until completely mixed in. Make a well in the centre and add the alcohol, lemon zest, egg and egg yolk. Whisk with a fork, bringing in a little of the flour at a time, until the dough is too stiff to work. Bring in the rest of the flour with your hands, then knead to bring the dough together. Continue to knead the dough for 6–8 minutes or until fairly smooth and quite stiff. If it is too crumbly and difficult to bring together, sprinkle in a little water, a teaspoon at a time, until the dough just comes together. Wrap in plastic wrap or baking paper and rest at room temperature for at least 30 minutes.

Meanwhile, combine all the blueberry compote ingredients in a saucepan. Stir well and cook over a medium heat for 8–10 minutes or until the blueberries have begun to collapse but still hold their shape and the syrup has thickened slightly. Allow to cool. (If the blueberries begin to collapse before the syrup has thickened, remove them with a slotted spoon and continue to reduce the syrup until thickened. Return the blueberries to the syrup and allow to cool.)

Working with one-quarter of the dough at a time (cover the remaining dough with an upturned bowl), use a pasta machine to roll out the dough. Roll the dough through a pasta machine through the widest few settings. Fold the dough into the centre from both of the shortest sides, like you're closing a book, then rotate it 90 degrees. Repeat this a few times through the first few settings. (The folding helps encourage the finished crostoli to be light, bubbly and crunchy.) Continue all the way to the thinnest setting until the dough is about 0.5 mm thick.

Using a fluted pastry cutter, cut the rolled-out dough into strips around 16 cm × 6 cm. Make a cut in the middle of each strip with the pastry cutter, then tuck the ends through the cut to make twirled ribbons.

My preference is to fry this batch immediately, as you don't want the dough ribbons to dry out, and then continue the rolling and folding once the first batch has been cooked. Alternatively, work in tandem and have someone frying and someone rolling.

Pour the vegetable or olive oil into a wok or saucepan to a depth of 7 cm and heat to 180°C or until a small piece of crostoli dough dropped in the oil browns in 15 seconds. Add the crostoli in batches and fry for 1–1½ minutes, turning halfway, until puffy and lightly golden. Transfer to paper towel to drain and cool.

Dust the crostoli with plenty of icing sugar and serve with the blueberry compote and a dollop of mascarpone.

SERVES 8

RASPBERRY TART

WITH ROSEMARY PASTRY CREAM

Reminiscent of the fruit tarts I love in Paris, this raspberry tart is very pleasing. I've flavoured the pastry cream with vanilla and rosemary, but a fresh bay leaf or some tarragon would be nice, too. It is not necessarily that it should taste of the herbs, but rather they should add a subtle herby earthiness to the custard. Both elements, the tart shell and pastry cream, can be made in advance and assembled at the last moment, just before serving.

375 g raspberries, halved

SWEET SHORTCRUST PASTRY

- 250 g (1⅔ cups) plain flour, plus extra for dusting
- 180 g cold unsalted butter, cubed
- 55 g pure icing sugar
- pinch of sea salt
- 1 egg

ROSEMARY PASTRY CREAM

- 6 egg yolks
- 130 g caster sugar
- 20 g plain flour
- 20 g cornflour
- 550 ml full-cream milk
- 1 rosemary sprig
- 1 vanilla pod, split and seeds scraped
- 2 tablespoons cold unsalted butter, cubed

For the sweet shortcrust pastry, place the flour, butter, icing sugar and salt in a food processor and pulse until the mixture resembles fine breadcrumbs. Add the egg and continue to pulse until the mixture just comes together. Turn out onto a work surface and gently shape into a disc, being careful not to overwork the dough. Wrap in plastic wrap or baking paper and refrigerate for 30 minutes or until nicely chilled but not too firm.

Roll the dough out on a lightly floured surface into a large disc about 3 mm thick, then carefully drape into a 24 cm round, fluted loose-based tart tin. Gently press the pastry into the edge of the tin, then trim the excess by pressing the top of the tin with a rolling pin. Prick the base of the tart all over with a fork, then place in the freezer for 20 minutes.

Preheat the oven to 190°C fan-forced.

Line the chilled tart shell with tin foil and fill with baking beads or uncooked rice or beans. Blind bake for 15 minutes, then reduce the oven temperature to 180°C fan-forced. Remove the tin foil and continue to cook for a further 15–20 minutes, or until it is an even golden colour all over. Allow to cool, then remove from the tin.

Meanwhile, to make the rosemary pastry cream, whisk the egg yolks, caster sugar, flour and cornflour in a large bowl. Combine the milk, rosemary and vanilla pod and seeds in a large saucepan and heat until just about to simmer. Add a little of the warm milk mixture to the egg mixture and whisk to combine. Continue pouring in the milk mixture and whisking until all is combined. Strain the mixture through a sieve, discard the rosemary and vanilla pod, then return the mixture to the same pan and cook, whisking constantly, over a medium heat for 3–4 minutes or until the custard is thick. Once the mixture comes to the boil, cook for a further 1–2 minutes. Transfer to a container and cover directly with baking paper (this stops a skin from forming). After 10 minutes, lift up the baking paper and whisk the butter into the pastry cream, one cube at a time. Refrigerate for at least 4 hours, but ideally overnight.

To assemble, whisk the pastry cream to loosen, then pipe or spoon the pastry cream into the baked tart shell. Top with the raspberry halves and serve.

SERVES 8–12

ME

NUS

MENU 01

Sweet days of summer

Summer is a time for celebration – Christmas, New Year – and new beginnings. It is also a time of long slow days spent between the beach, afternoon naps and reading outside in the cool of the evening. No one is in a hurry for anything at all. This translates to easy outdoor cooking and having friends over for relaxed meals. The outside grill gets utilised more in these months than any time throughout the whole year and I often build a menu around this. Charring eggplants until blackened and soft, lamb is marinated the day before and simple salads are tossed together. A strawberry cake to finish because the strawberries are just so good right now.

MENU 02

Salt water & market memories

ITALIAN ABUNDANCE

After spending a month in Puglia, Italy, I came home with not just new ideas and inspiration, but a feeling of lightness and a renewed sense of generosity. Travel does that I think, but, in particular, it is the people. New friends who I cooked and ate with and the vivacious fruttivendoli, who will happily peel you something to try on the spot, or fill your arms with local oranges to take with you. I love market shopping in Italy. But if I don't have cooking facilities and am only looking, there is much longing. When I can settle into a town, have a little kitchen to cook in, and really shop like a local, it is magic. This is a menu inspired by that lightness. It is one for hot weather cooking.

MENU 03

Grape leaves & wild herbs

A SENTIMENTAL FEELING

This is a true feast – large plates of food, generous and satisfying. Big flavours, mess and happiness. Whenever I cook a whole fish, I feel like I'm a little girl again. It reminds me of family dropping by with a fish they have just caught. My mum preparing it, then cooking it for everyone. Instead of serving it Maltese style, as my mum would, I wrap it in grape vine leaves before roasting and serving it with salmoriglio that I make with wild Sicilian oregano. The boldness of the za'atar chicken is a fine addition to the feast. Sesame flatbread to mop everything up, a fresh salad and breakfast (bougatsa is traditionally served with your morning coffee) for dessert.

MENU 04

Pure comforts

HAPPY IN WINTER

The oven is on, there are pots bubbling on the stove and rain streaks all the windows. A warmth comes from the kitchen and the ingredients lend themselves to slow cooking, hearty meals and pure comfort. This is a menu that requires a little time, because when it is dreary outside, I can think of nothing more pleasant than pottering around in the kitchen – rubbing pastry, stirring polenta and making madeleines.

MENU 05

Warm enough to eat outside

When the chill of winter is no longer and new peas, zucchini flowers and the first of the berries begin to appear, cooking a meal and eating it outside feels momentous. Perhaps some blankets at the ready are still necessary, but you're outdoors and it is glorious. I love spring cooking, it is so colourful, bright and joyful.

Mozzarella, crème fraîche &
boiled lemon __ 40

Stracci with zucchini & their flowers __ 70

King George whiting with braised peas
& tarragon __ 112

Crostoli with mascarpone &
blueberry compote __ 224

Magic beans & chestnuts

AN ELEGANT LUNCH TO SHARE WITH FRIENDS

The first borlotti beans of the season usually come in early autumn. Chestnuts are there, plums, too. I begin to pod the beans and they show what they are made of – deep hues of magenta to pale crimson speckles mottle the tan-coloured beans. Once cooked, they are more a greyish-brown, but they don't lose their magic. I invite friends over for a Sunday lunch. It is a celebration with a white linen tablecloth and tall beeswax candles. We begin with small bowls of the minestra and finish with the light and airy torta paradiso and an espresso.

MENU 07

A celebration of citrus

I keep a large antique bowl I bought in Italy on my bench. It is the citrus bowl and is always filled with lemons, limes and oranges. They are as important to my cooking as good olive oil and salt. This is a menu that celebrates a love for citrus – from the prawns that are marinated in lemon slices and aromatics, to the portokalopita that benefits from the whole orange. Bitterness, sweetness and texture.

MENU 08

Sumac & saffron

A simple dinner made for my family on a rather lovely spring day. The cake is a particular show stopper – damp and fragrant, it is a wonderful end-of-meal treat. To make this menu more substantial, serve the lamb with sesame flatbread (see page 27), too.

Marinated spiced lamb with cucumber yoghurt — 134

Zucchini, broad bean & freekeh salad — 165

Pistachio saffron cake with lemon saffron icing — 204

MENU 09

I cannot really think of a city I love as much as Rome and so I often feel rather nostalgic for my time there. This nostalgia is expressed in the kitchen, where I dig through the notebooks and menus I have kept from my travels, looking to make something that will take me there. Food is wonderful like that. I made this meal on a Saturday night – tomatoes on toast ready as people arrived, cake cooling, potato and silverbeet al forno in the oven. This is how I like to cook when friends come over. Just one or two things needing attention so I can enjoy the meal as much as my guests.

MENU 10

I really don't like fussy food. For me, simple is always best. Simple is also special. New season peas and broad beans were the starting point for this meal, then I decided on some delicate homemade pasta with the most fragrant fish filling. It sets the tone for the lunch. Simple yet special. The pork is served to much delight and, at the very last moment, the tart is assembled and served. A very pleasurable way to eat.

MENU 11

A lovely dinner with friends

I began this menu with the apricots. I had bought plenty at the market and my plan to serve them simply with some mascarpone and crushed pistachios was foiled. They were not sweet enough yet. Plans changed for the better after I macerated them in sugar and turned them into a tart – so jammy and delightful. Now that dessert was sorted, I decided to serve lamb meatballs with a punchy sauce, roasted fennel with cherry tomatoes and some pizza bianca as a snack. A snack is always a good idea when you have people over. It takes the pressure off you in the kitchen and allows you to feel in control.

MENU 12

Cool weather cooking

After a few hot skin-prickling months, while I lament a little for the summer stone fruit and juicy mangoes, I am relieved to jump into some cooler weather cooking. Glorious cabbages of varying greens, motley pumpkins and jewel-like rhubarb are at their best and make for a soft landing as the days get shorter. Eating outdoors is no longer, instead we settle into the dining room for the next little while. On the table is a warming soup, deep orange and rich. A stuffed cabbage that looks nothing short of a painting. A creamy rice pudding served warm, to really let you know the season. There is beauty in this kind of cooking. It is understated, familiar and makes for a very pleasant dinner.

Pumpkin & sage soup with mascarpone ___ 61

Stuffed cabbage with sausage & porcini ___ 126

Creamy rice pudding with rhubarb, raspberries & cardamom ___ 217

CONVERSION CHARTS

Measuring cups and spoons may vary slightly from one country to another, but the difference is generally not enough to affect a recipe. All cup and spoon measures are level.

One Australian metric measuring cup holds 250 ml (8 fl oz), one Australian metric tablespoon holds 20 ml (4 teaspoons) and one Australian metric teaspoon holds 5 ml. North America, New Zealand and the UK use a 15 ml (3-teaspoon) tablespoon.

LENGTH

METRIC	IMPERIAL
3 mm	⅛ inch
6 mm	¼ inch
1 cm	½ inch
2.5 cm	1 inch
5 cm	2 inches
18 cm	7 inches
20 cm	8 inches
23 cm	9 inches
25 cm	10 inches
30 cm	12 inches

LIQUID MEASURES

CUP	METRIC	IMPERIAL
⅛ cup	30 ml	1 fl oz
¼ cup	60 ml	2 fl oz
⅓ cup	80 ml	2½ fl oz
½ cup	125 ml	4 fl oz
⅔ cup	160 ml	5 fl oz
¾ cup	180 ml	6 fl oz
1 cup	250 ml	8 fl oz
2 cups	500 ml	16 fl oz
2¼ cups	560 ml	20 fl oz
4 cups	1 litre	34 fl oz

One American pint = 500 ml (17 fl oz)
One Imperial pint = 600 ml (20 fl oz)

DRY MEASURES

METRIC	IMPERIAL
15 g	½ oz
30 g	1 oz
60 g	2 oz
125 g	4 oz (¼ lb)
185 g	6 oz
250 g	8 oz (½ lb)
375 g	12 oz (¾ lb)
500 g	16 oz (1 lb)
1 kg	32 oz (2 lb)

The most accurate way to measure dry ingredients is to weigh them. However, if using a cup, add the ingredient loosely to the cup and level with a knife; don't compact the ingredient unless the recipe requests 'firmly packed'.

OVEN TEMPERATURES

CELSIUS	FAHRENHEIT
100°C	200°F
120°C	250°F
150°C	300°F
160°C	325°F
180°C	350°F
200°C	400°F
220°C	425°F

METRIC	IMPERIAL
110°C	¼
130°C	½
140°C	1
150°C	2
170°C	3
180°C	4
190°C	5
200°C	6
220°C	7
230°C	8
240°C	9
250°C	10

THANKS

To my book village, the dream team who helped bring this book to life, an enormous thank you. I feel so lucky to work with you all and I am very grateful for all of your hard work, guidance and skill on this book.

Mary Small, Clare Marshall, Armelle Habib, Michelle Mackintosh, Karina Duncan, Megan Johnston, Sarah Watson, Meryl Batlle, Kimberlea Smith, Rufus Cuthbert and Charlotte Ree.

To my wonderful agent, Alexandra Neville, thank you for all of your amazing support, kindness and advice.

To Andy, Mitch and Bruce, for having us in your beautiful space to shoot the cover, I am immensely grateful for your generosity.

Thank you to Jamie Furlan and Danni Sollier from LNDN for making my hair look a million bucks and Karen Burton for the cover day makeup!

To Oliver and Lisa from Ramarro Farm for the most beautiful produce for the shoot and also over the years. So many recipes are inspired by your produce. Thank you!

To my friends and family, especially my mum, Rachel, and sister, Sarah, who have helped me immensely while I wrote and shot this cookbook. I appreciate all of your feedback, patience and support.

To Julie and Francesco, for opening your home and heart to me while in Puglia. A special time spent together, which was both rejuvenating and inspiring. Grazie.

To my cousin Joanna in Malta, thank you for your generous hospitality and warmth. To know that I come from such a long line of wonderful cooks was very special to discover.

Roberta, Luca and Benedetta, my second family. Grazie mille! Whenever I spend time with you all, I learn so much and feel so inspired. I feel so fortunate that our paths crossed all those years ago.

To Nori, Haruki and Yukito. The best people in my life and my whole world. Thank you for cheering me on every single day and for being the most encouraging yet discerning taste testers. Love you all and love cooking with, for and around you.

INDEX

D

E

F

G

R

S

T

U

W

Y

Z

Pan Macmillan acknowledges the Traditional Custodians of Country throughout Australia and their connections to lands, waters and communities. We pay our respect to Elders past and present and extend that respect to all Aboriginal and Torres Strait Islander peoples today. We honour more than sixty thousand years of storytelling, art and culture.

A PLUM BOOK
First published in 2024 by
Pan Macmillan Australia Pty Limited
Level 25, 1 Market Street,
Sydney, NSW 2000, Australia

Level 3, 112 Wellington Parade,
East Melbourne, VIC 3002, Australia

Designed by Michelle Mackintosh
Typeset by Megan Ellis
Edited by Megan Johnston
Index by Helen Holmgren
Photography by Armelle Habib
Food and prop styling by Karina Duncan
Food preparation by Meryl Batlle, Julia Busuttil Nishimura and Sarah Watson
Colour reproduction by Splitting Image Colour Studio
Printed and bound in China by 1010 Printing International Limited

A CIP catalogue record for this book is available from the National Library of Australia.

10 9 8 7 6 5 4 3 2 1